SIL LUM KUNG-FU
THE CHINESE ART OF SELF-DEFENSE

LEO T. FONG

EMPIRE BOOK/AWP LLC
Los Angeles, CA.

DISCLAIMER

Please note that the author and publisher of this book are NOT RESPONSIBLE in any manner whatsoever for any injury that may result from practicing the techniques and/or following the instructions given within. Since the physical activities described herein may be too strenuous in nature for some readers to engage in safely, it is essential that a physician be consulted prior to training.

First Revised Edition published in 2022 by AWP LLC/Empire Books.
Copyright (c) 2022 by AWP LLC/Empire Books.

All rights reserved. No part of this publication may be reproduced or utilized in any form or by any means, electronic or mechanical, including photo- copying, recording, or by any information storage and retrieval system, without prior written permission from AWP LLC/Empire Books.

EMPIRE BOOKS
P.O. Box 491788
Los Angeles, CA 90049

First revised edition
Library of Congress Catalog Number: ISBN-13: 978-1-949753-84-4
22 21 20 19 18 17 16 15 14 13 12 11 10
Library of Congress Cataloging-in-Publication Data
Siu Lum Kung Fu by Fong Leo -- Revised ed. p. cm.

ISBN 978-1-949753-84-4 (pbk. : alk. paper) 1. Kung fu. 5. Martial arts-- technique. 3. Large type books. I. Title. GV1114.3.F715 20148861.815'3--dc22
2006014411
Printed in the United States of America.

Acknowledgements

I wish to express my sincere appreciation to Mr. Ed Ikuta for the excellent photography and to my dear and loyal friend Richard Garvey for his willingness to pose for the pictures in the section on "breakdown". My apology to Mr. Garvey for the few stray kicks and punches which did not miss their mark.

PREFACE

The martial arts of Judo, Karate, Aikido and Kendo have grown rapidly in the United States during the last ten years. Kung-Fu, however, has not grown in proportion to other martial arts due to the adherence by many of its sifu (instructors) to the old prejudice of anti-Occidentalism with respect to their art. This unwillingness to reveal the subtleties of the art is understandable since when Kung-Fu was first developed, the Chinese civilian population practiced its techniques secretly, passing them only from father to son or, at most to other close family member, Gradually, Kung-Fu was passed to all relatives with the same surname. It has only been in the last few years that sifu who depend upon the teaching of the art for a living have found it necessary to open their Kwoon (schools) to "outsiders" in order to survive economically. Still, the number of these sifu, compared to the number that still behold Kung-Fu as a dark secret, is minute.

This book is being written with several purposes in mind. An art that is kept secret might have a certain amount of public appeal but also attracts a considerable number of pseud-masters and phonies who are in a perfect position to exploit the innocent and uninformed. Exposure can help develop greater appreciation and understanding of the art.

Kung-Fu is not a deadly art superior to Karate, Judo, Boxing or Aikido. It is only as effective as the one practicing it. A 90-year-old, 110-pound man with a knowledge of Kung-Fu may not always win in an encounter with a 175-pound uninformed, untrained street fighter. The elder Kung-Fu practitioner's success will depend upon his ability to move and evade, to keep calm and think, to strike and punch with authority, to maintain stamina and endurance in the encounter. His ability to maintain a psychological edge will determine the final outcome.

This book contains some of the basic exercises for the learning of the Sil Lum system of Kung-Fu. However, more important than tangible techniques is one's mental attitude. Any training that does not embody discipline and humility is ineffective. The mastering of circumstances and the winning of respect from others depend upon the mastering of one's own self. It is hoped that the physical art of this book will open the door to the spiritual art.

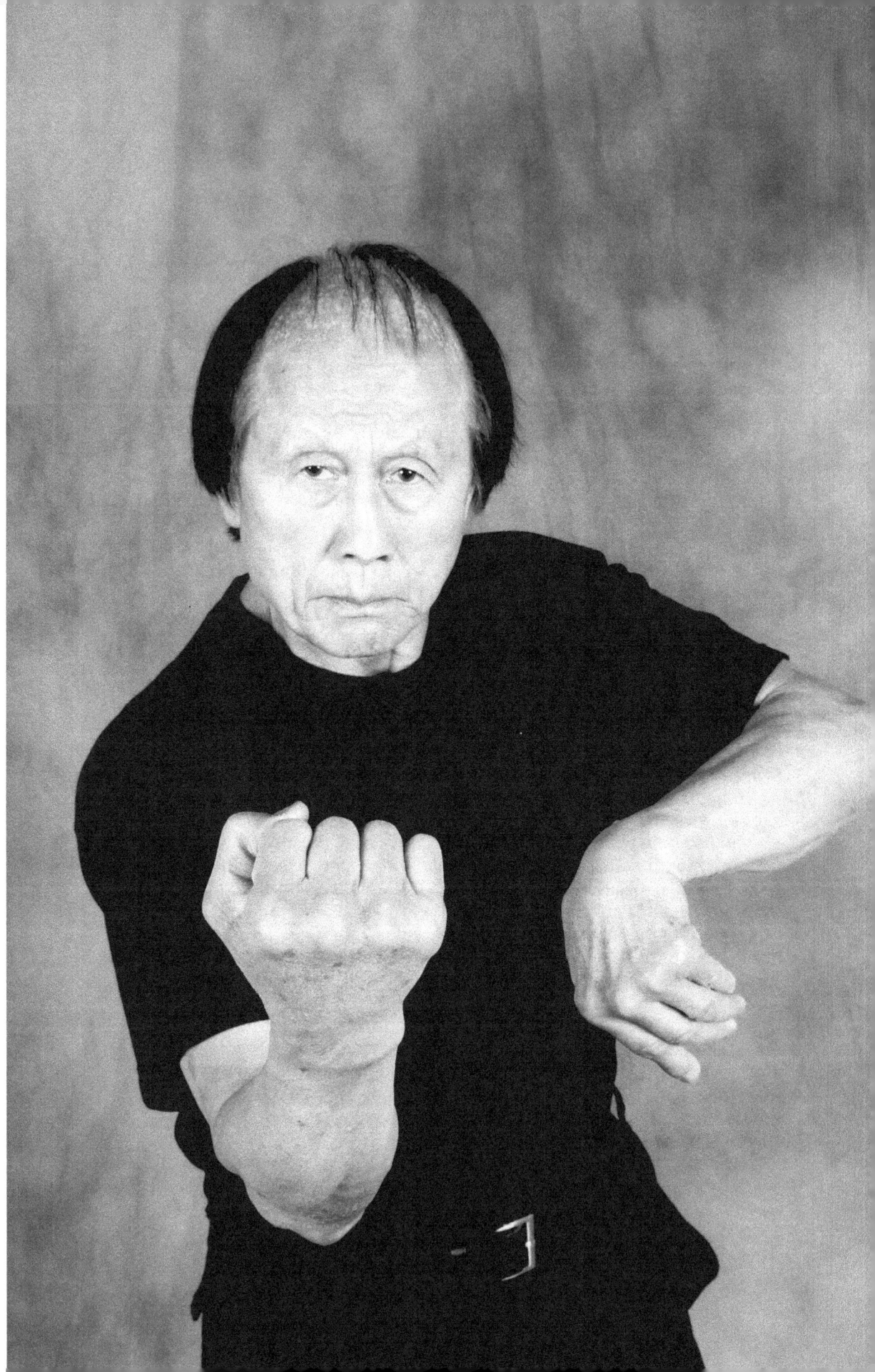

DEDICATION

In the last two and a half years I have realized several dreams. Of those is the publishing of a book on Kung-Fu. This fulfillment would not have been possible without the encouragement and inspiration of my wife. It is to Libertad S. Fong that I humbly dedicate this first volume.

ABOUT THE AUTHOR

LEO TIM FONG was born in Canton, China in 1929 but immigrated to the United States with his parents when he was only five years old. By the time he had reached high school age, Mr. Fong had found sports—including track and tennis, football and boxing—to be a way of life. In fact, his training with gloves at Hendrix College in Conway, Arkansas proved to be much more than an energy-charged outlet from studies, and he was proclaimed the 1949-51 collegiate boxing champion and a 1950-52 Arkansas AAU finalist.

A degree in physical education was followed by study at Southwestern Methodist University (Texas) where Mr. Fong fought his way to the Southwestern Golden Gloves finals. But his physical education was behind him. Now he was working toward a degree in theology, the first in a long series of steps to reach the people around him.

As a minister in Sacramento, California, Mr. Fong hoped to dissolve the boundaries between the pulpit and parishioners, particularly those lines seemingly separating the Church from its children. What good was theory if it didn't relate to actual experience? So he worked to find a viable means of communica-

ting with young people in a way which they could understand and be willing to accept.

Mr. Fong found that the martial arts gave him the opportunity to reach people in a way the Church could not. His extensive training in Judo, Ju-Jitsu, Tae Kwan Do and Kung-Fu gave him a tangible means of expressing what words could not portray.

Today the author is not preaching but, rather, sharing his 12 years of practical experience in Sil Lum Kung-Fu with students of all ages. And they listen.

CONTENTS

Brief History of Kung-Fu 12

Tips for Using This Book 15

Warm-Up Exercises 17

Pictorial Glossary of Blocks and Strikes 39

Horse Stance Training 55

Lin Wan Kune Form Practice 61

Lin Wan Kune Complete 121

Application of the Form 137

The Evolution of the Integrated Fist 161

A BRIEF HISTORY OF KUNG-FU

The exact origins of Kung-Fu are not known. Down through the centuries many nations have claimed techniques as their own and have offered colorful, if sometimes contradictory, legends to prove their claims. To give a complete and accurate history of Kung-Fu would be impossible due to records lost and destroyed during the antiquity of time. However, Kung-Fu historians believe that the art emigrated from India to China around the year 525 A.D.

Legend has it that Daruma Taishi journeyed to China to instruct the Liang Dynasty in the tenets of Buddhism. Upon his arrival in China, after having traveled hundreds of miles through the rugged Himalaya Mountains, he purportedly imposed such rigid discipline and harsh pace on his student monks that they collapsed one by one from sheer physical and mental exhaustion. In subsequent sessions Daruma was said to have pointed out to the students that although Buddhism places great emphasis on the spirit and salvation of the soul, the body and soul are inseparable. The physical condition has much effect upon the status of the spirit. In their weakened condition they could never perform the ascetic discipline required to reach a state of true enlightenment.

According to legend, Daruma began to teach members of the Sil Lum (*Shaolin* in Mandarin) monastery a form of physical and mental exercises called *Eki-Kinkyo* to strengthen the body and mind, not only for self-defense purposes when defending themselves against armed marauders in their itineracy from one location to another, but also as a vehicle to reach greater spiritual heights.

Another legendary pioneer and outstanding exponent of the Sil Lum system of Kung-Fu was a monk by the name of Leong Sil Jung. Sil Jung entered the Sil Lum monastery at the age of ten years. After spending some 50 years in meditation and training of the mind, body and spirit, it was said that he descended from the monastery to teach in the world. Shortly thereafter he entered Woung-Nam Province and learned about a wealthy nobleman who had been searching for a competent Kung-Fu teacher for his frail and sickly son, Hue Lung Gong.

The Chinese Art of Self-Defense

Upon meeting the father, Sil Jung consented to teach the boy. The father built a school and for the next ten years his son practiced Sil Lum Kung-Fu under the expert tutelage of Leong Sil Jung.

Following the death of his master at the age of 80 years, Hue Lung Gong became a teacher and one of his foremost students was Leong Tin Chee, the nephew of Leong Sil Jung. The meeting of student and teacher had been coincidental. Leong Tin Chee had heard from traveling merchants that his uncle was teaching in Woung-Nam Province and had hoped to fulfill a life-long ambition to study under his famous relative. Although he was saddened to learn of his uncle's death, Leong Tin Chee remained in Woung-Nam and, until he was 40 years old, studied under Hue Lung Gong.

Having completed his training, Leong Tin Chee returned to his native Kwang-Sai Province to teach. Traveling from province to province, he opened many schools where his skill as a teacher was in great demand. One of his most promising pupils was Wong Tim Yuen who studied under Leong Tin Chee for ten years. When Wong Tim Yuen came to the United States at the age of twenty-six, he was the first known practitioner to bring the Sil Lum system of Kung-Fu.

The self-defense movements of Sil Lum resemble those of various animals whose methods of fighting inspired the intricate martial arts techniques—"Monkey Grabbing the Peach", "Nine Dragons at Sea", "Tiger Descending the Mountain", "Bear Crossing the Bridge". Each technique, broken down and practiced for application, can be quite effective in combat or physical conditioning.

The word *Sil Lum* means "young forest". A young forest has resilience—its limbs can give with a strong wind and rebound with force. Thus is the essence of the art of Sil Lum Kung-Fu. Kung-Fu does not advocate meeting the opponent's force with force. Its basic philosophy emphasizes the ideal of giving with the adversary, to bend slightly and spring back stronger than before, to adapt oneself harmoniously to the opponent's movements without striving or resisting.

TIPS FOR USING THIS BOOK

Kung-Fu is as much mind as it is body. Concentration is an indispensable and integral part of Kung-Fu training. Each movement is designed for a purpose—to block or parry an attack and to ready for a counterattack.

Before each training session, warm up with a reasonable amount of the basic exercises, then practice two or three movements from the form. Repeat these same movements daily for one week before proceeding to the next sequence. Practice all the movements slow and fast, soft and hard.

Know the first form completely before you begin the applications, but do not attempt to learn all the forms at once. It is better to master two movements perfectly than to learn a thousand haphazardly. Remember: the effectiveness of Sil Lum Kung-Fu depends upon split-second timing and reflexive action, which are achieved only through repetitious practice.

When performing the movements, always use your imagination. Picture your adversary attacking, and use the Kung-Fu techniques in response to this imagined attack. As these techniques become more innate, new meaning will begin to emerge and better techniques can be formulated.

Before you begin with your training, read the following sections through a couple of times to get a general idea of the movement, particularly the form, and the direction in which each technique is executed. You are entering into an art, but more than that, a constructive way to acquire confidence, not only in facing an adversary, but also in meeting life's challenges and problems. Kung-Fu, if practiced diligently and constructively, can be a vehicle toward a keen mind, a healthy body and a positive attitude. Good luck with your training!

WARM–UP EXERCISES

Warm-up exercises are an integral part of Kung-Fu training. The muscles of the body are susceptible to injuries when they are not thoroughly warmed up and limber.

The exercises in this section have been selected to prepare the body for an often strenuous application of techniques.

Arm-and-Leg Stretching Exercise

Stand upright with your legs spread apart. Inhale as you slowly raise your hands upward until they are slightly over your head. Then exhale as you

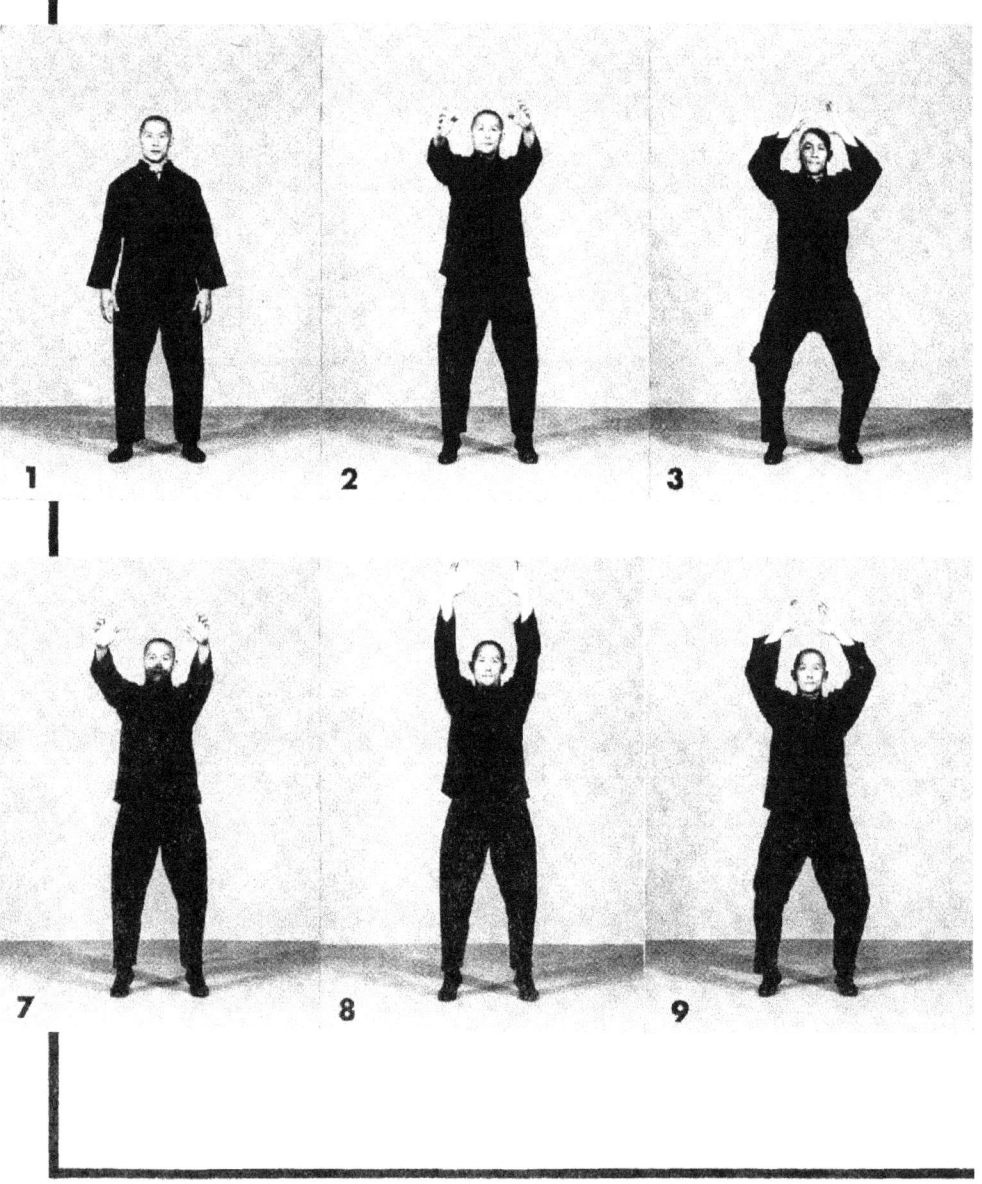

slowly squat to the floor, your hands fully extended. Inhale as you slowly return to an upright position, raising your hands until they are fully extended above your head. Exhale as you slowly squat to the floor, arms fully extended at your sides. Return to an upright position as you complete the cycle. Repeat the cycle 10 to 20 times.

Abdominal Exercise

Stand upright with your legs spread apart. Bounce your upper torso three times toward the floor, then stretch three times backward. Repeat the exercise 10 to 20 times.

The Chinese Art of Self-Defense

Leg Stretching Exercise

Crouch as low to the floor as possible with one leg stretched out, and push down on your knee three times. Alternate the exercise with your other leg and repeat it 10 to 20 times.

Leg and Abdominal Exercise

Sit on the floor with your legs spread and hands grasping your ankles. Bend forward on three counts and then return to an upright position. Repeat 10 to 20 times.

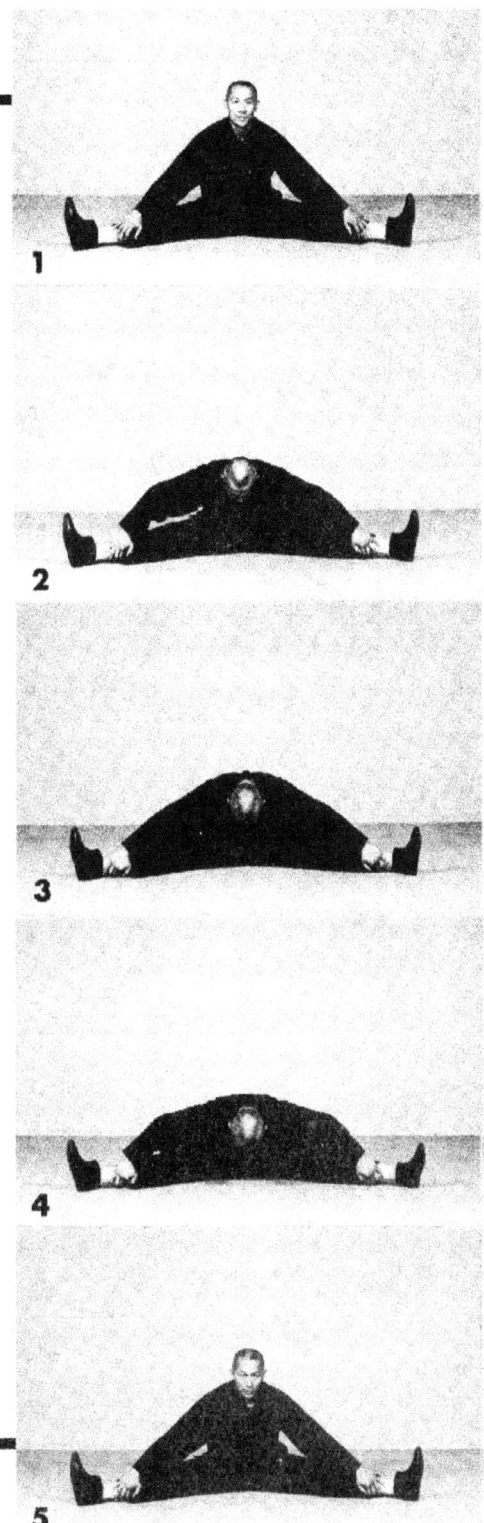

Squat and Jump Exercise

Stand upright with your legs spread slightly apart and hands at your sides. Squat with your buttocks and thighs relaxed, then tense your buttocks and thighs as you jump up.

Front Kick Exercise

Stand upright with your legs spread slightly apart and hands at your sides. Place one hand straight out in front of you, and kick with the opposite leg until your foot touches your hand. Keep the rest of your body as stationary as possible. Alternate hand and leg, and repeat the exercise 10 to 20 times on each leg.

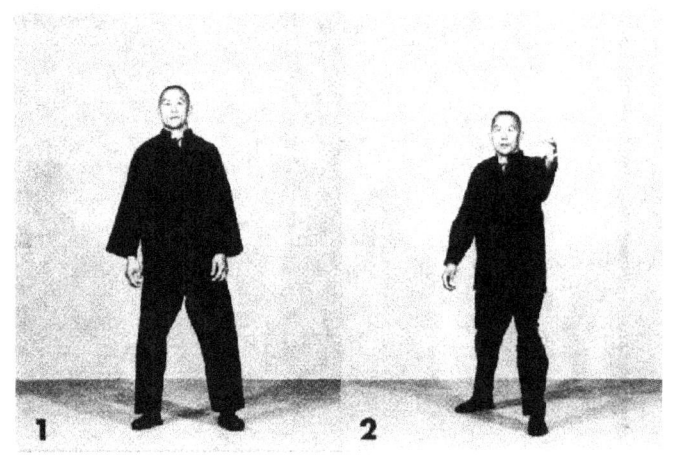

High Front Kick Exercise

Stand upright with your legs spread slightly apart. On the count of one, lift one leg waist-high. Immediately lift the same leg head-high or higher on the count of two. Always keep your leg straight and knee locked. Repeat the exercise with your other leg.

The Chinese Art of Self-Defense

Leg Exercise with Partner

Stand as erect as possible. Grasp your partner's left shoulder with your right hand. He should then grasp your right shoulder with his left hand. On the count of one, he should hold your outstretched right leg at waist level, pushing it to shoulder level on the count of two and finally to head level, or maximum height, on the count of three. Return to your original position and reverse the leg.

Fingertip Push-Up Exercise

Put yourself in a push-up position, using your fingertips at the base instead of your palms. Keep your back straight and inhale as you lower your body to the floor, then exhale as you return to your original position.

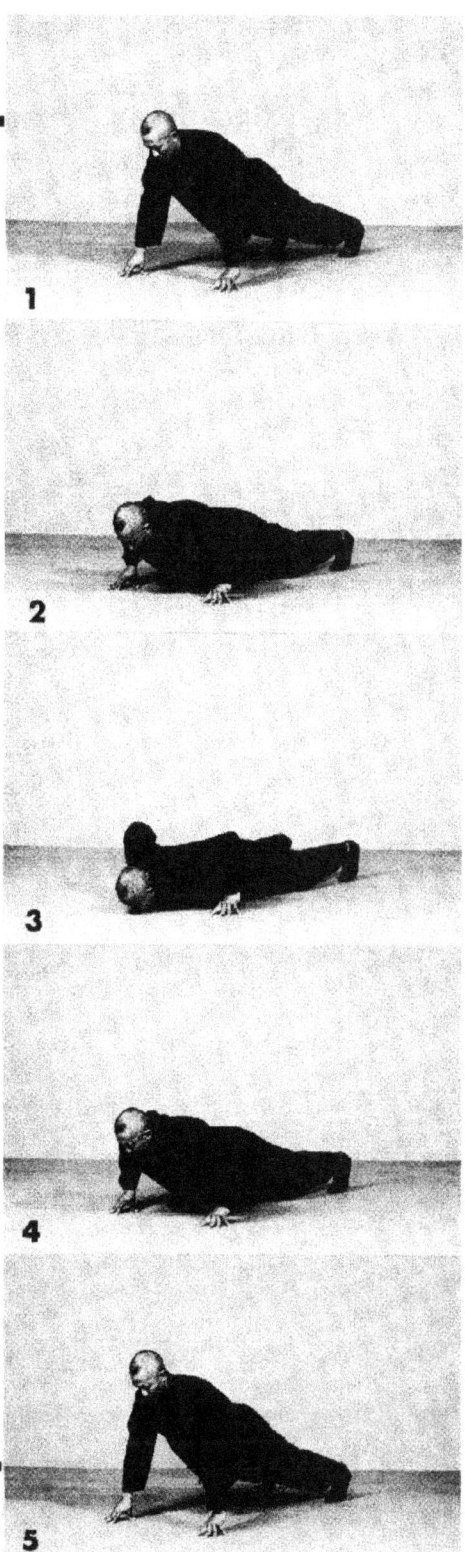

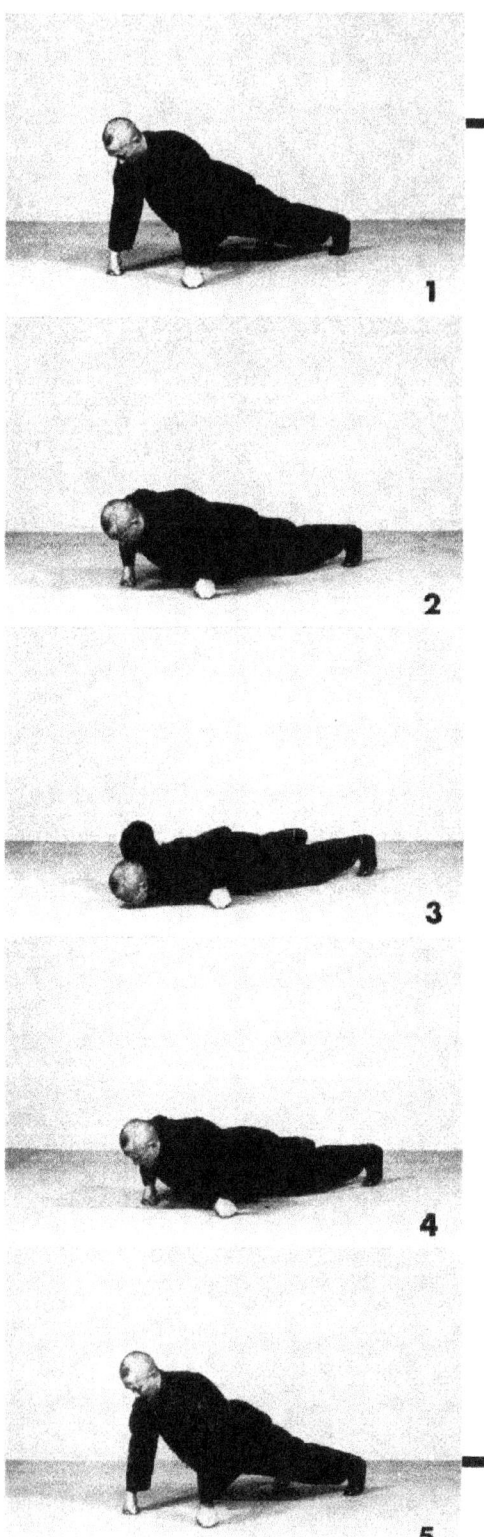

Knuckle Push-Up Exercise

Put yourself in a push-up position, using your knuckles at the base. If the floor is hard, use a towel as padding until your knuckles harden. Keep your back straight and inhale as you lower your body to the floor, then exhale as you return to your original position.

One-Hand Knuckle Push-Up Exercise

Put yourself in a one-hand, push-up position, using your knuckles at the base instead of your palm. Place the other hand on your hip. Keep your back straight and inhale as you lower your body to the floor, then exhale as you return to your original position. This exercise requires strength and balance and, so, may be difficult for the beginner. But it can be accomplished by practicing the two-hand push-ups regularly.

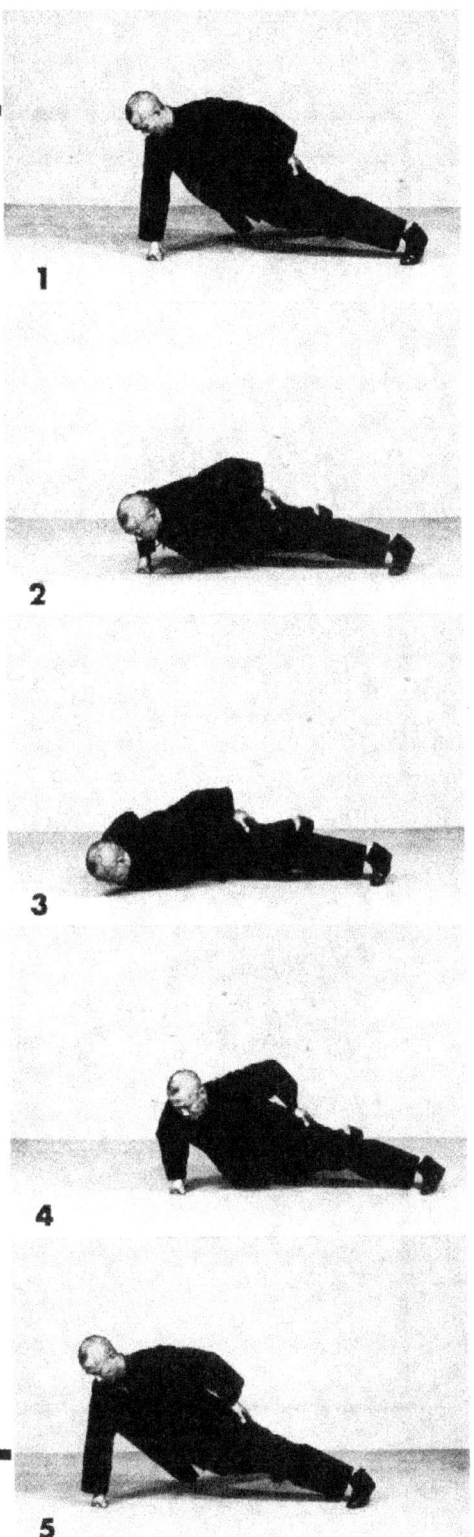

SIL LUM KUNG-FU

Rotating Push-Up Exercise

This exercise is done in a rotating motion. Put yourself in a regular push-up position, but spread your legs wide apart. Slowly lower your head and upper torso toward the floor as close to your feet as possible, forcing your hip

The Chinese Art of Self-Defense

up. Move your face close to the floor in a rotating manner, as if your nose is almost scraping it, then push your face as far in front as possible and slowly return to the original position. Repeat the cycle 10 to 20 times.

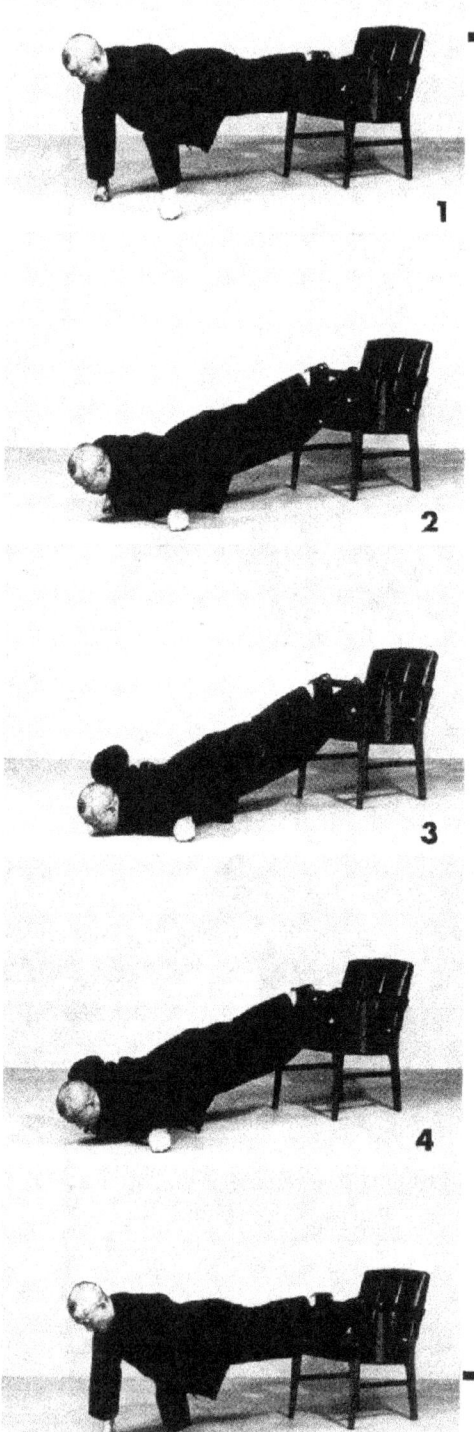

Elevated-Feet Knuckle Push-Up Exercise

Use a chair to support your feet, then do the two-hand knuckle push-up. The chair seat should be high enough so your body will be level. Keep your back straight and inhale as you lower your body to the floor, then exhale as you return to your original position.

Abdominal Leg-Raise Exercise

Lie flat on your back with your legs extended and your hands at your sides. Slowly raise your knees and head until the knees reach your chest. Return to the original position.

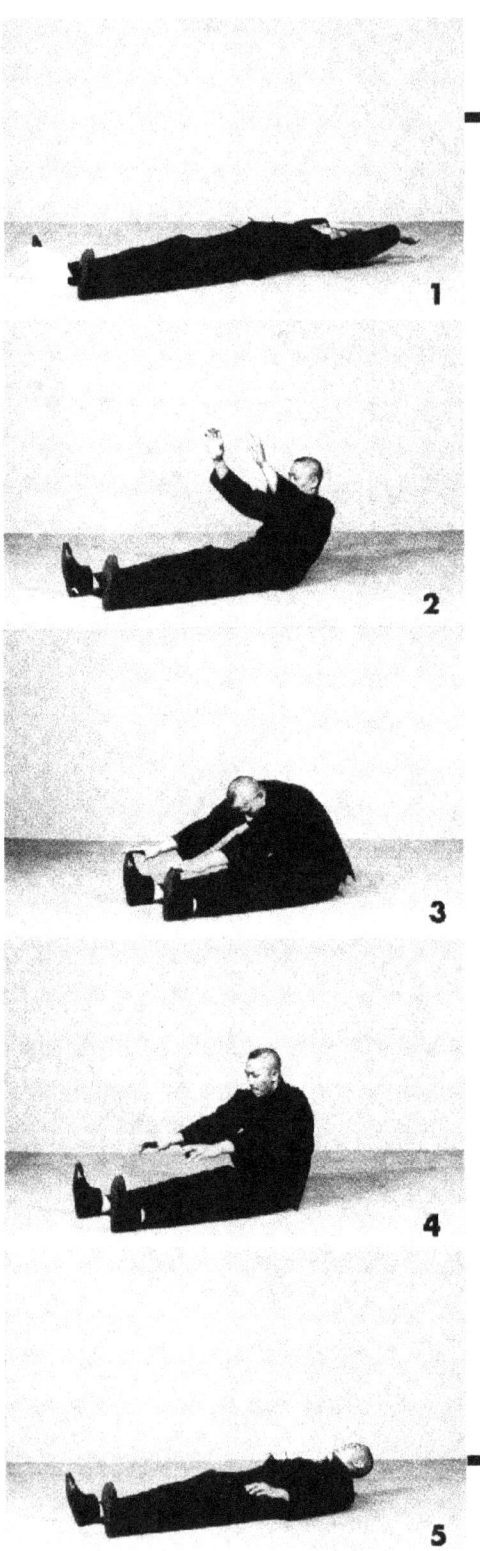

Sit-Up Exercise

Lie flat on your back with your legs slightly apart and your hands extended over your head. Slowly bring your hands forward and simultaneously lift your head and body until your hands touch your toes. Slowly return to the original position. Repeat the cycle 10 to 20 times.

Leg-Raise Exercise

Lie flat on the floor with your feet slightly apart. Slowly raise your knees to the chest, then straighten out and return to your original position. Repeat the exercise 20 to 30 times.

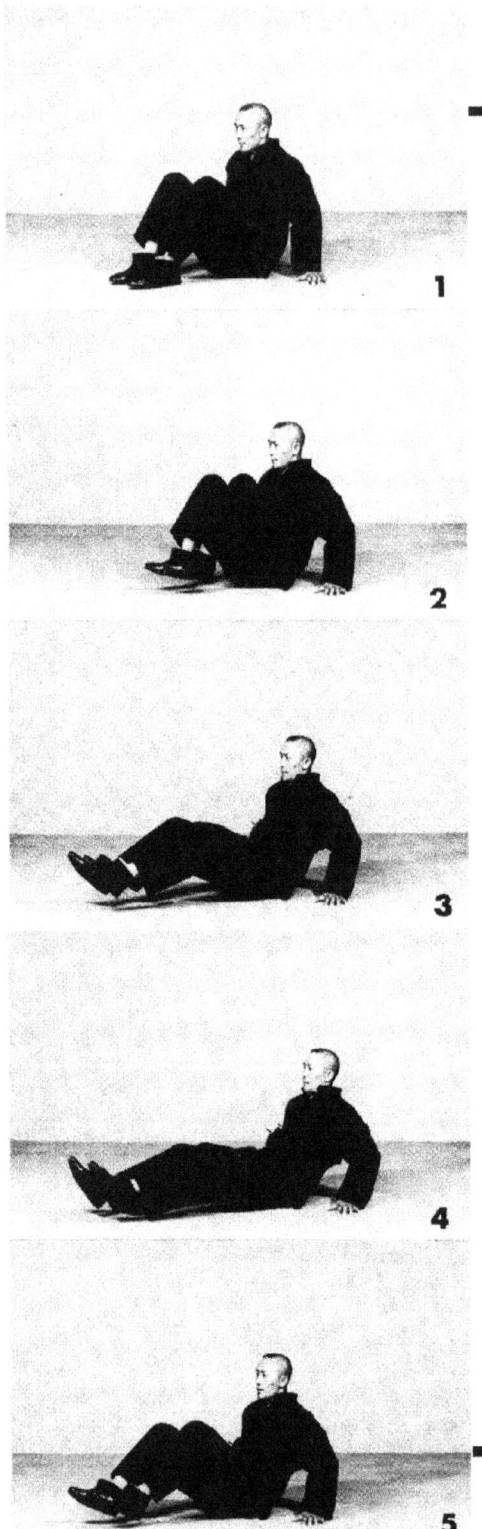

Abdominal Sitting Exercise

Sit on the floor with your knees up, feet flat and hands down. Keep your palms on the floor and bring your knees to the chest. Slowly straighten your legs and hold them just ¼ inch off the floor. Return to original position and repeat the exercise 20 to 30 times.

Bench Sit-Up Exercise

Sit on a stool or box with your hands held behind your head. Have a sparring partner hold your ankles while you slowly bend backward as far as possible. Slowly return to the original position.

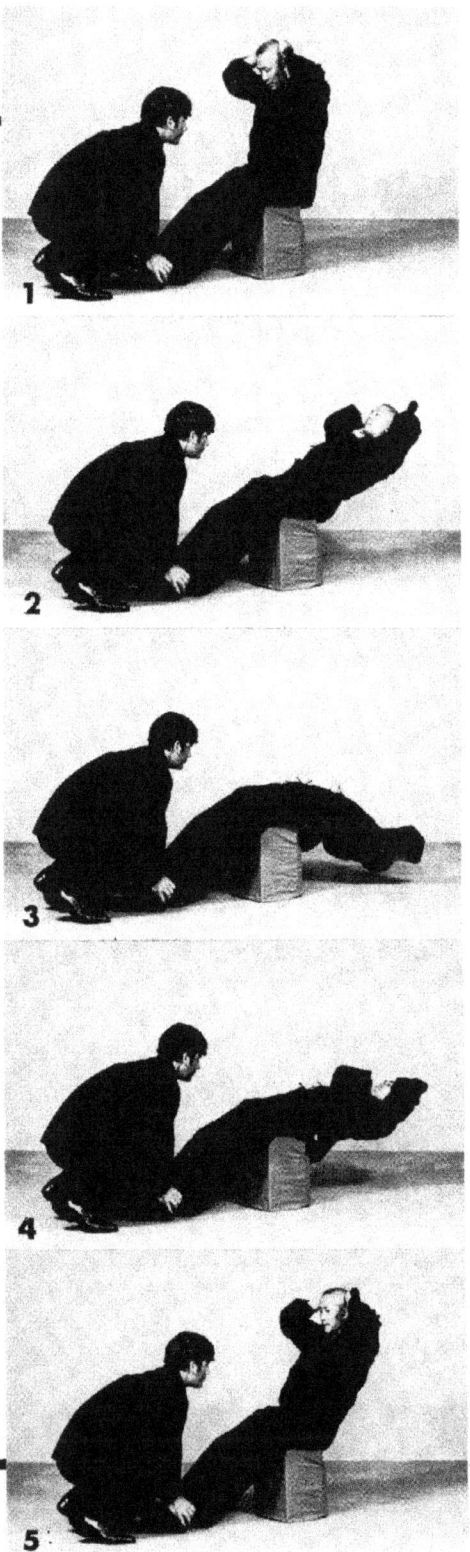

PICTORIAL GLOSSARY OF BLOCKS AND STRIKES

Familiarity with the contents of this section will be helpful in performing the form "LIN WAN KUNE" or the Continuous and Returning Fist. Perfecting single basic blocks and strikes can be helpful in execution and comprehension of the breakdowns for defense and attack. Application depends greatly on the perfection of single basic motions.

THE SLICE BLOCK "Serc Gort"

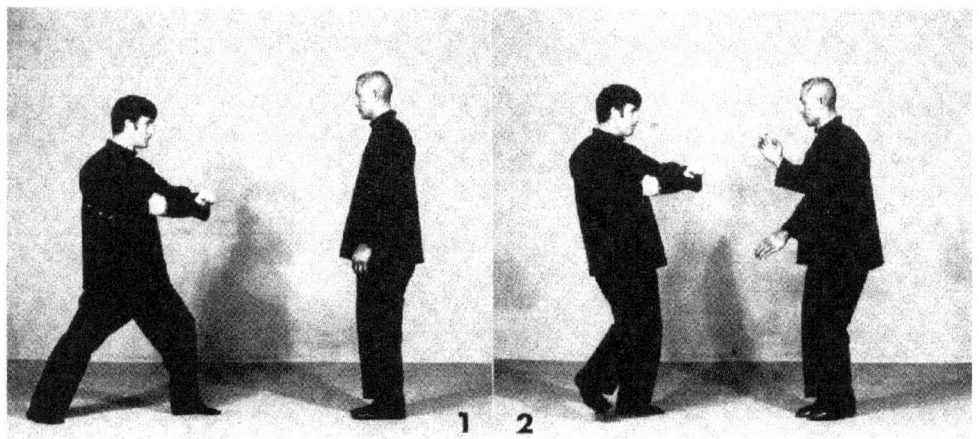

To block and sweep a front kick, simultaneously raise your right arm and step back with the left foot, then slice your arm downward to sweep your opponent's foot. Counter Defense: the opponent is vulnerable to a punch to the kidney and choke from the back.

INSIDE LOWER BLOCK "Noy Gort"

To block a low, front kick, step back with your left foot and simultaneously block with your forearm. Counter Defense: opponent is vulnerable to a front snap kick to the groin or a back fist strike to the temple.

The Chinese Art of Self-Defense

INSIDE MIDDLE BLOCK
"Noy Gort"

To block a straight punch, step back and simultaneously raise your arm to parry the blow with the forearm. Counter Defense: opponent will be vulnerable to a hammer fist counter to the groin or a fore-fist rake strike to the face.

CIRCULAR BLOCK
"Wu Won Gort Yiet"

To block a straight punch from the opposite side, step to your left and bring your right arm up high in an upward arc to stop his blow. Counter Defense: grab the opponent's arm with your right hand and punch to his kidneys with your left (not shown).

SINGLE FLYING-FOOT KICK
"Fay Gerk"

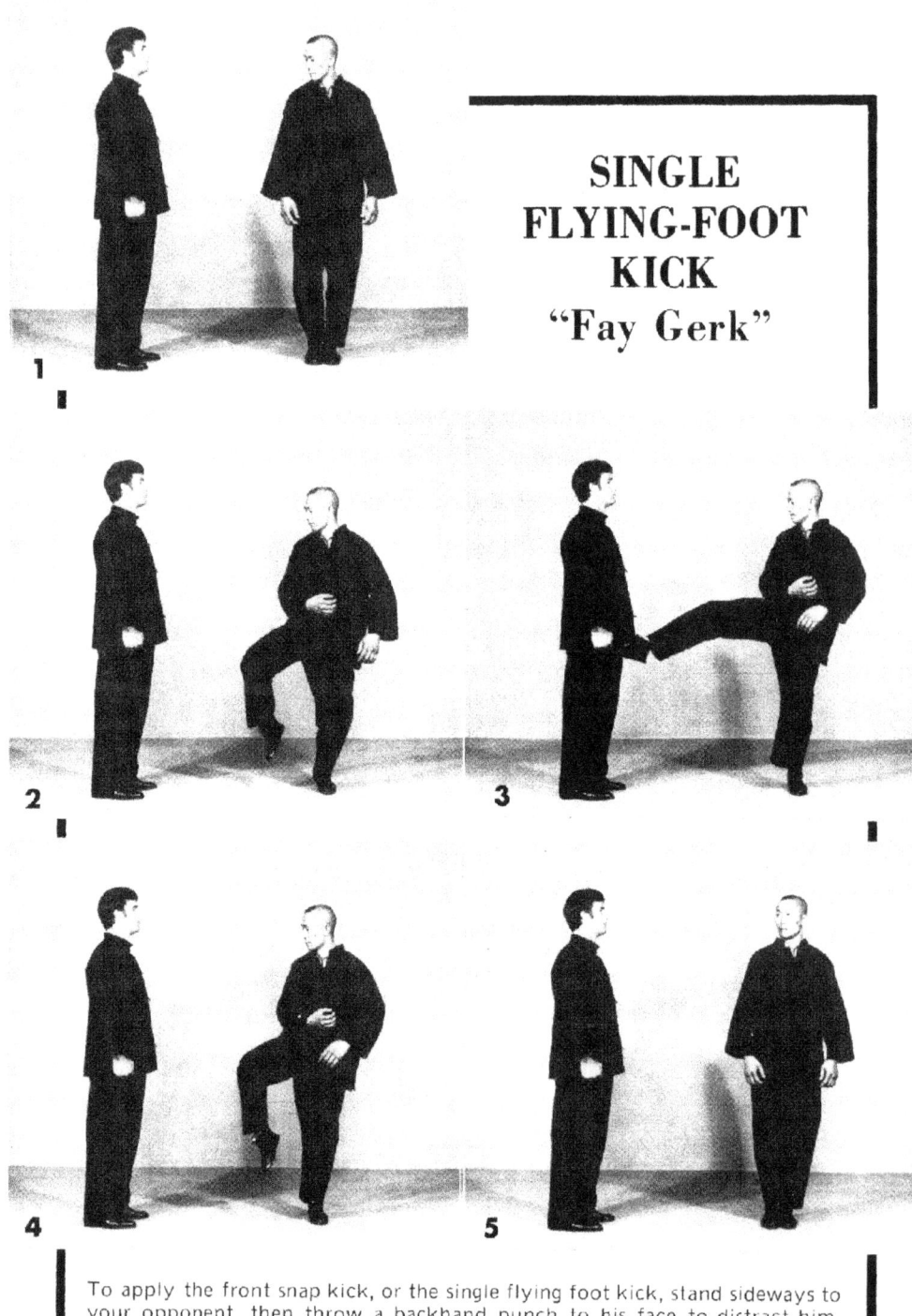

To apply the front snap kick, or the single flying foot kick, stand sideways to your opponent, then throw a backhand punch to his face to distract him. Raise your knee slightly and apply a front snap kick to his groin, knee or shin.

CANNON PUNCH
"Pow Choy"

To apply the cannon punch, face your opponent sideways with your feet together. Then step forward with your right foot and simultaneously strike with a finger jab to his face or throat. Immediately apply an uppercut to his chin or lower ribs by twisting your hip as your left hand returns to its original position.

1

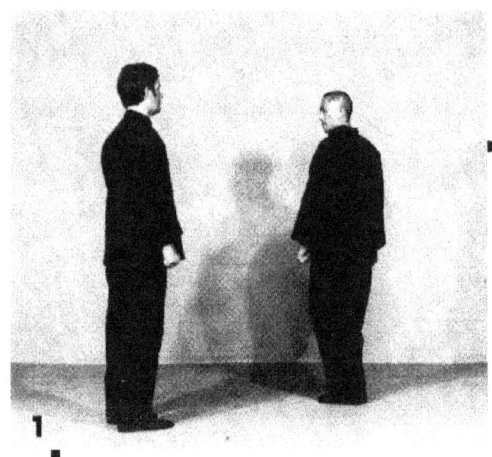

DRAGON HEAD PUNCH
"Lung Tow"

2

3

4

5

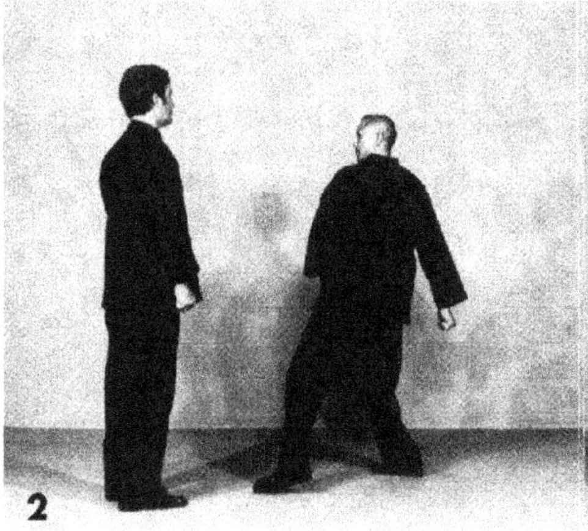

To apply the dragon head punch, twist your body back, extending the right hand. Then swing your arm with full force to your opponent's temple or eye. The fist must be clenched with the middle knuckle protruding.

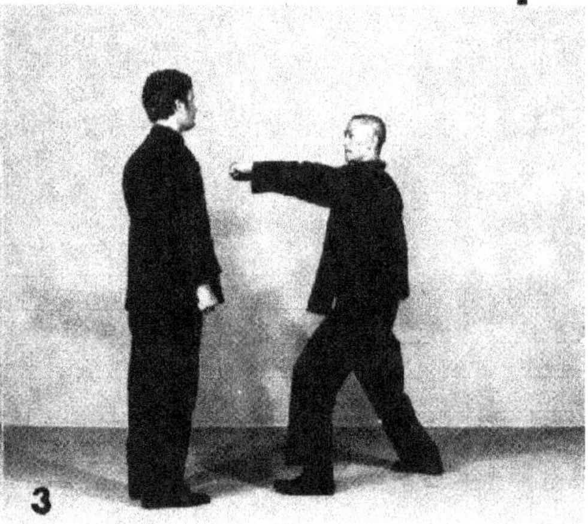

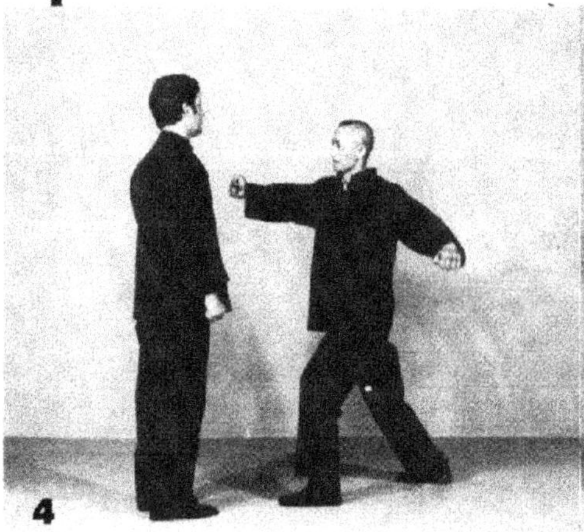

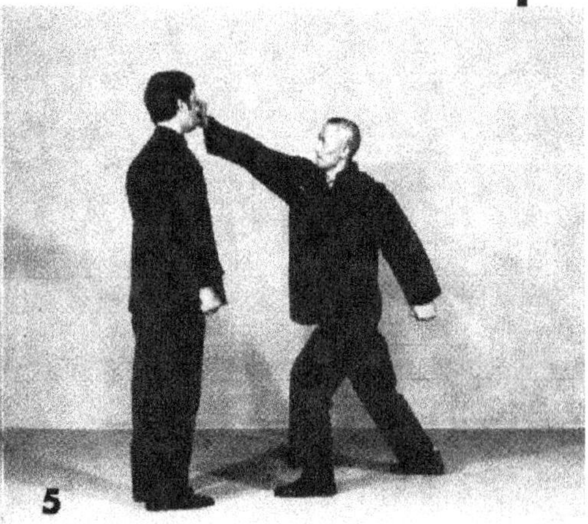

UPPERCUT ELBOW STRIKE
"Jang Tow"

To apply the uppercut elbow strike, face your opponent sideways with your feet together. Then step forward with your right foot and simultaneously strike with a finger jab to his face or throat. Immediately swing your body in with an elbow strike to the chin by twisting your hip as the left hand returns to its original position.

LATERAL ELBOW STRIKE
"Jang Tow"

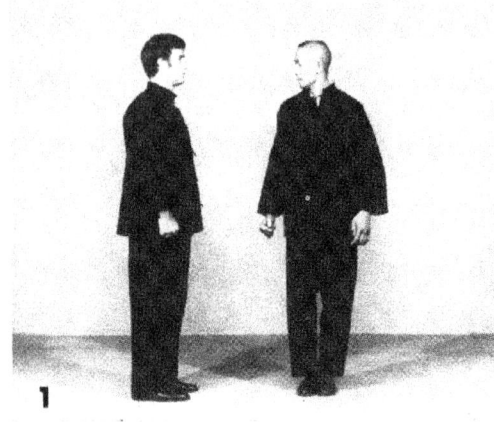

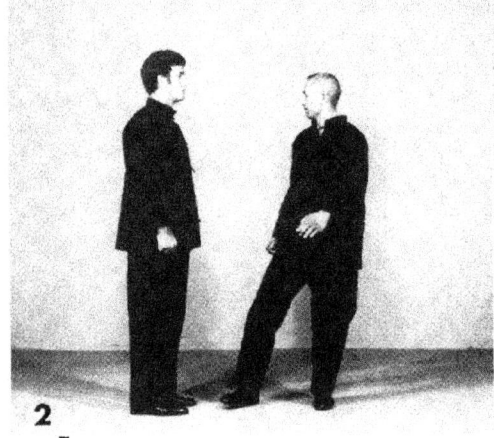

To apply the lateral elbow strike, face your opponent sideways with feet together. Then step forward with the right foot and simultaneously strike with a finger jab to the throat. Follow up with a lateral elbow strike to the jaw or lower ribs by twisting your shoulders.

BACK FIST
"Qua Choy"

To apply the back fist, face your opponent sideways with feet together. Step forward with the right foot, clenching your right hand and raising your left arm to your shoulder to protect yourself from any blow. Swing your right hand to the head, temple, jaw or bridge of your opponent's nose.

REVERSE PUNCH "Ping Kune"

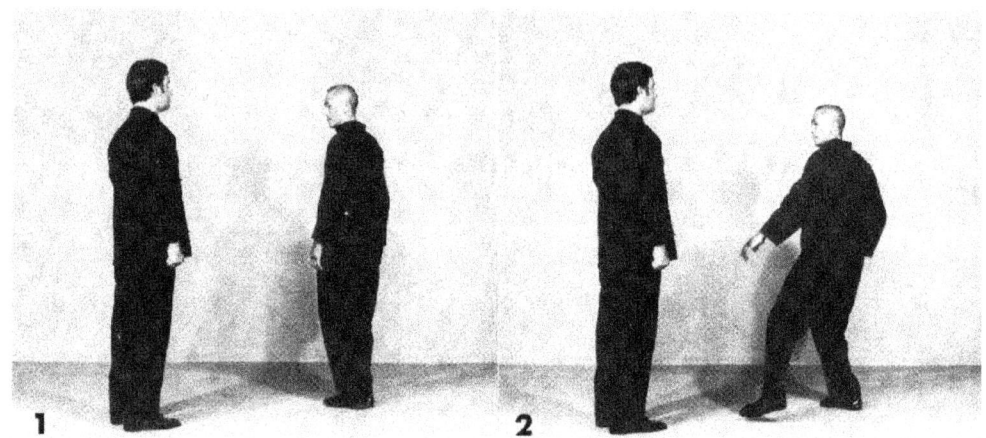

To apply the reverse punch, face your opponent sideways with your left foot closest to him. Step toward him with your left foot. Raise your left arm to protect your body and simultaneously apply a reverse punch to the upper part of his body by twisting your entire body into the blow.

CIRCULAR HAMMER FIST "Sot Kil"

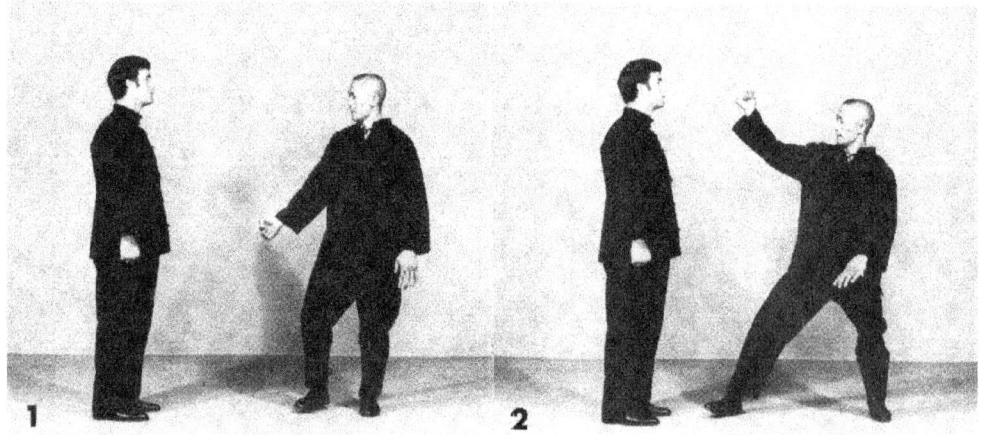

To apply the circular hammer fist, face your opponent sideways, feet together. Step forward, raise your right hand to eye level and follow through in a counterclockwise motion, delivering the blow to the groin.

The Chinese Art of Self-Defense

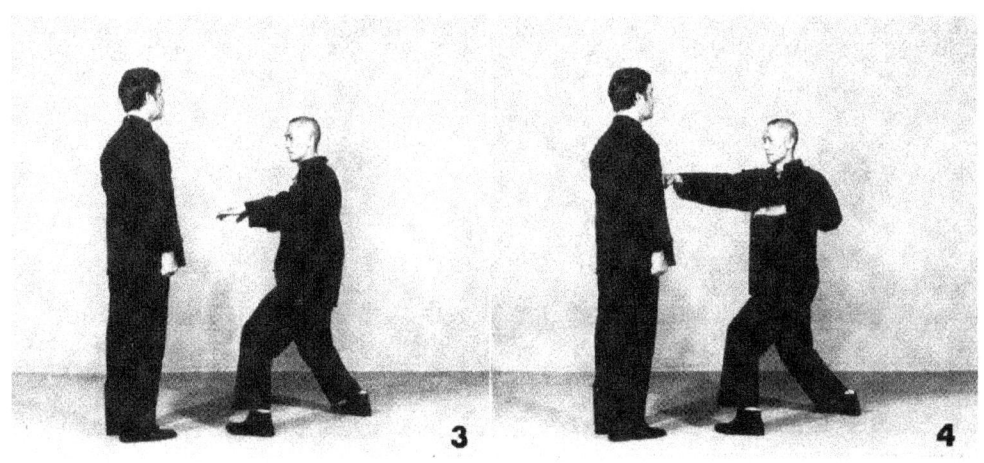

FOUR FINGER JAB "Bul Jee"

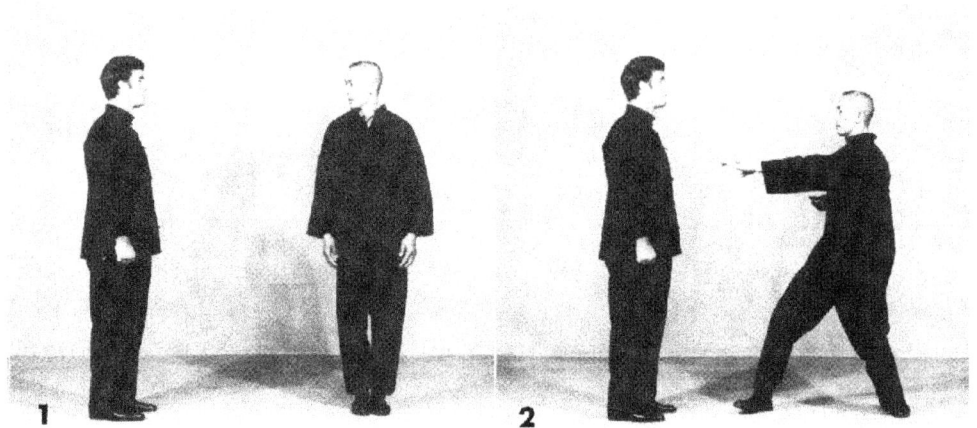

To apply the four finger jab, face your opponent sideways, feet together. Step off with the right foot, and as you raise your left arm to protect your body, jab with your right hand to the eyes.

TIGER CLAW "Foo Jow"

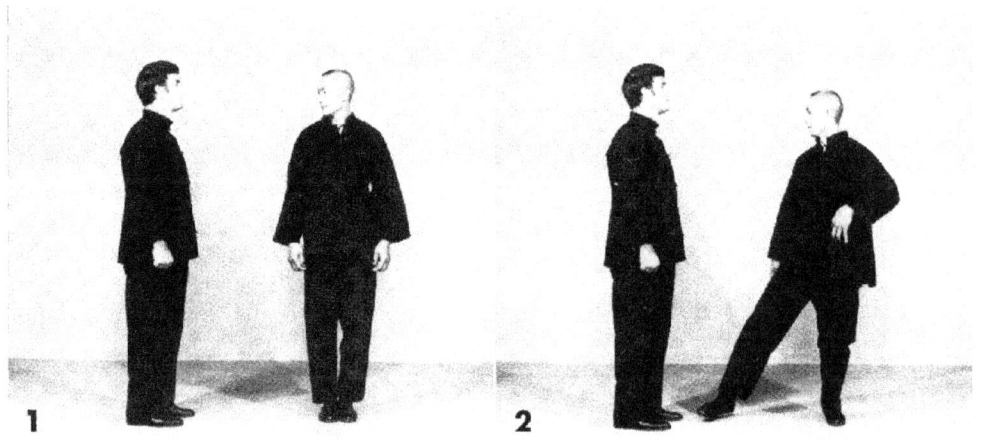

To apply the tiger claw, face your opponent sideways, feet together. Step off with your right foot and simultaneously lift your left arm, striking and clawing the face and eyes.

The Chinese Art of Self-Defense

HORSE STANCE TRAINING

The foundation of Kung-Fu is in the legs. Therefore, the value of Jop Mah—the horse stance—training cannot be overemphasized. The old masters believed that a solid stance contributes to the power needed for the execution of the various techniques. The square horse training in the following section seeks to accomplish two things: development of mobility and solidarity. Solidarity without mobility results in slowness of execution and failure to close the gap. Mobility without solidarity results in lack of power and focus. The correct positioning of the horse is necessary prior to executing other Sil Lum Kung-Fu techniques.

SIL LUM KUNG-FU

(1) Stand with your legs together, knees slightly bent and fists at waist-level. (2) Step to the left with your left foot. (3) Assume a horse stance with your weight equally distributed on both legs. (4) Pivot left on your left foot and (5) then place your right foot parallel to your left in a circular movement.

The Chinese Art of Self-Defense

(The distance between both feet must always be the same when placing your right foot in alignment with your left in a circular movement. See Diagram 5A.) You are now faced 90 degrees from your original position. (6) Assume a second horse stance. (7) Pivot to the left with your left foot.

SIL LUM KUNG-FU

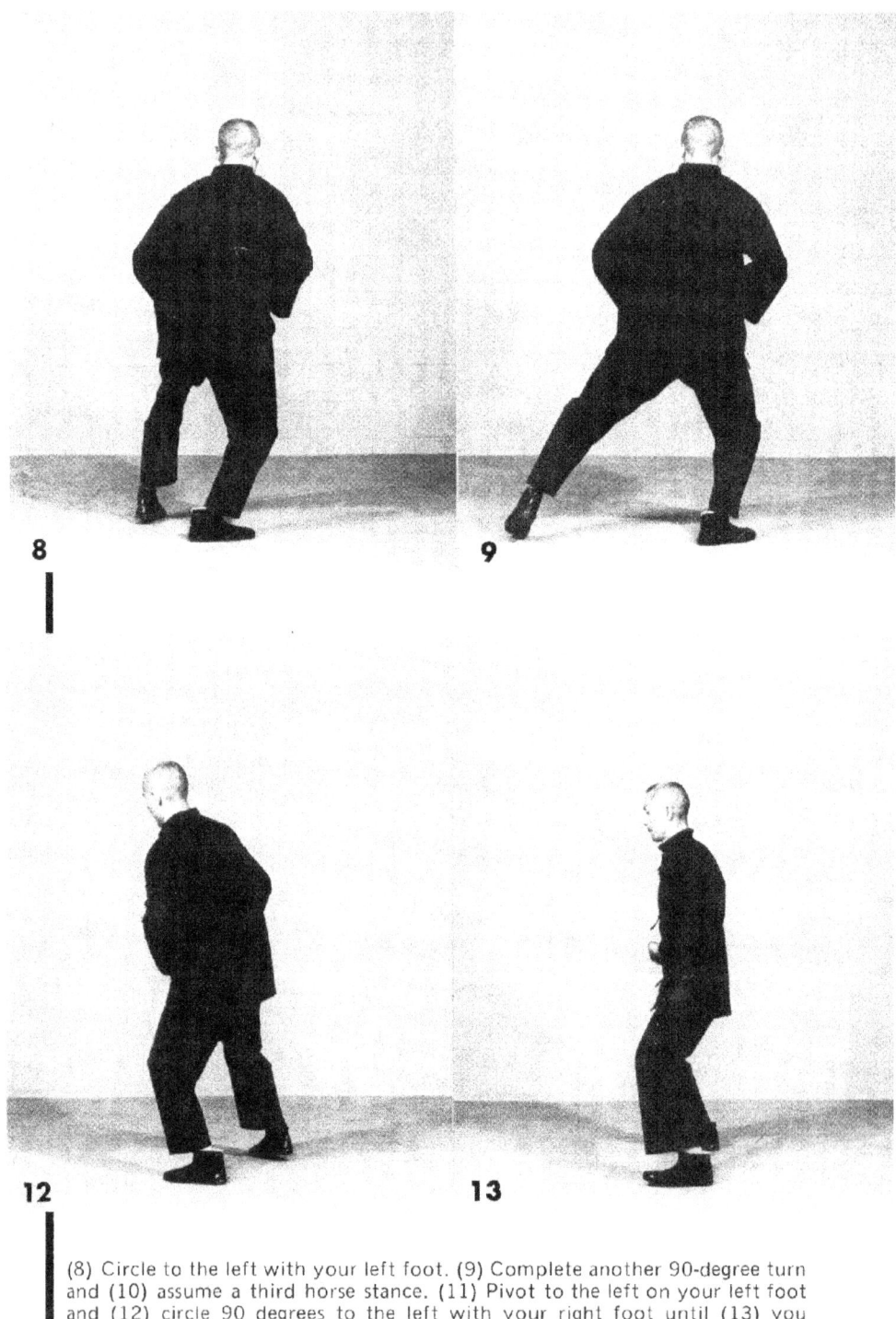

(8) Circle to the left with your left foot. (9) Complete another 90-degree turn and (10) assume a third horse stance. (11) Pivot to the left on your left foot and (12) circle 90 degrees to the left with your right foot until (13) you arrive in a fourth horse stance. (14) Circle 90 degrees to the left with your

The Chinese Art of Self-Defense

left foot and (15) return to your original horse-stance position. This exercise should also be practiced in a clockwise direction as well as the counter-clockwise direction shown.

LIN WAN KUNE FORM PRACTICE

Form practice is an integral part of the art of Sil Lum Kung-Fu training. Each movement of **Lin Wan Kune**—the continuous and returning fist—is designed for defense, counter and attack. The main purpose of form practice is to develop coordination, fluidity, speed and familiarity with Sil Lum combination techniques. Concentration and imagination are of the utmost importance for the maximum benefit. The best method of learning this basic form is to study the photographs thoroughly and to practice two to three movements at a time. Repeat the same motions daily for a week before proceeding to the next.

OPENING THE HORSE

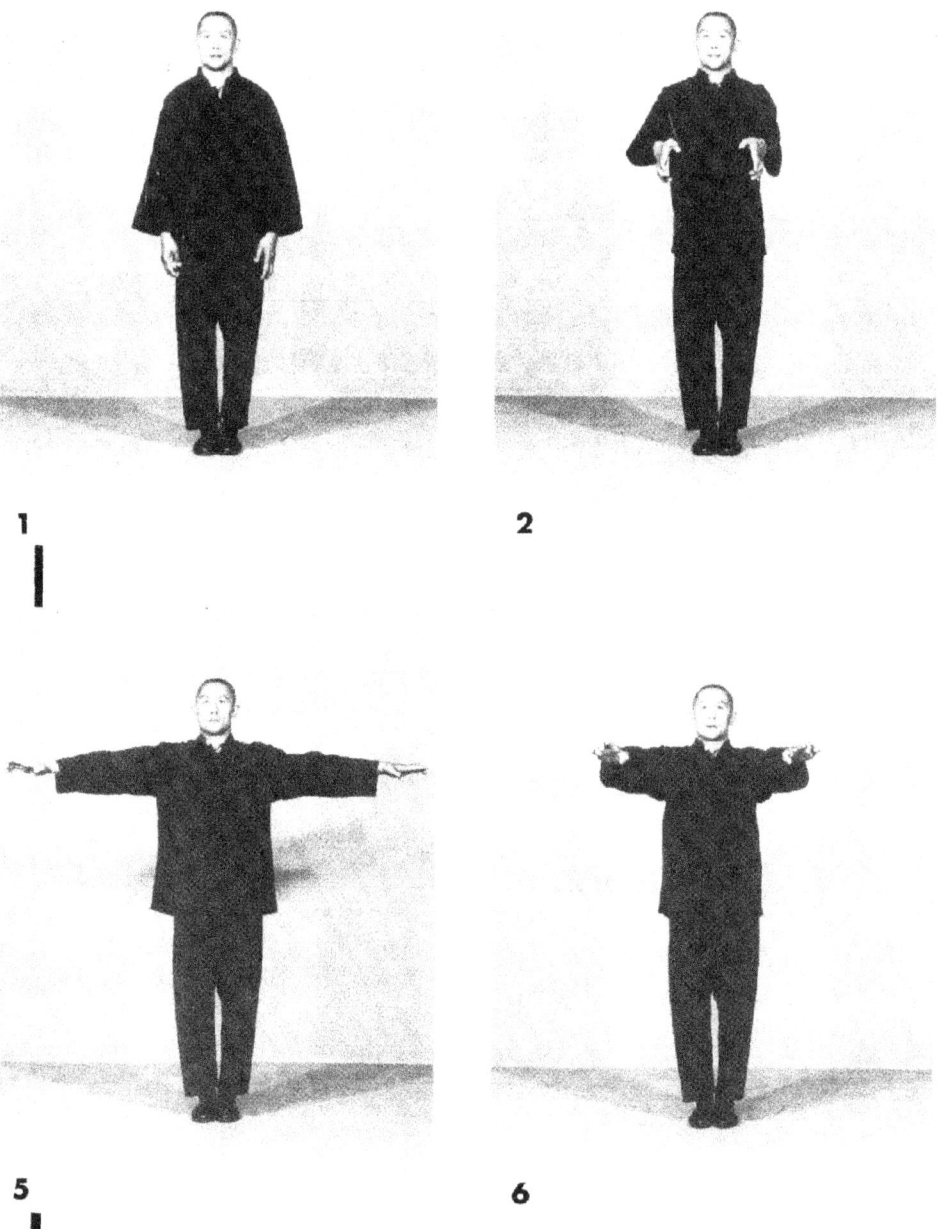

(1) Stand at attention with your feet together and arms at your sides. (2) With palms and fingers facing each other, slowly raise your hands past your chest to (3) shoulder-level. (4) Turn your palms downward, slightly curving

The Chinese Art of Self-Defense

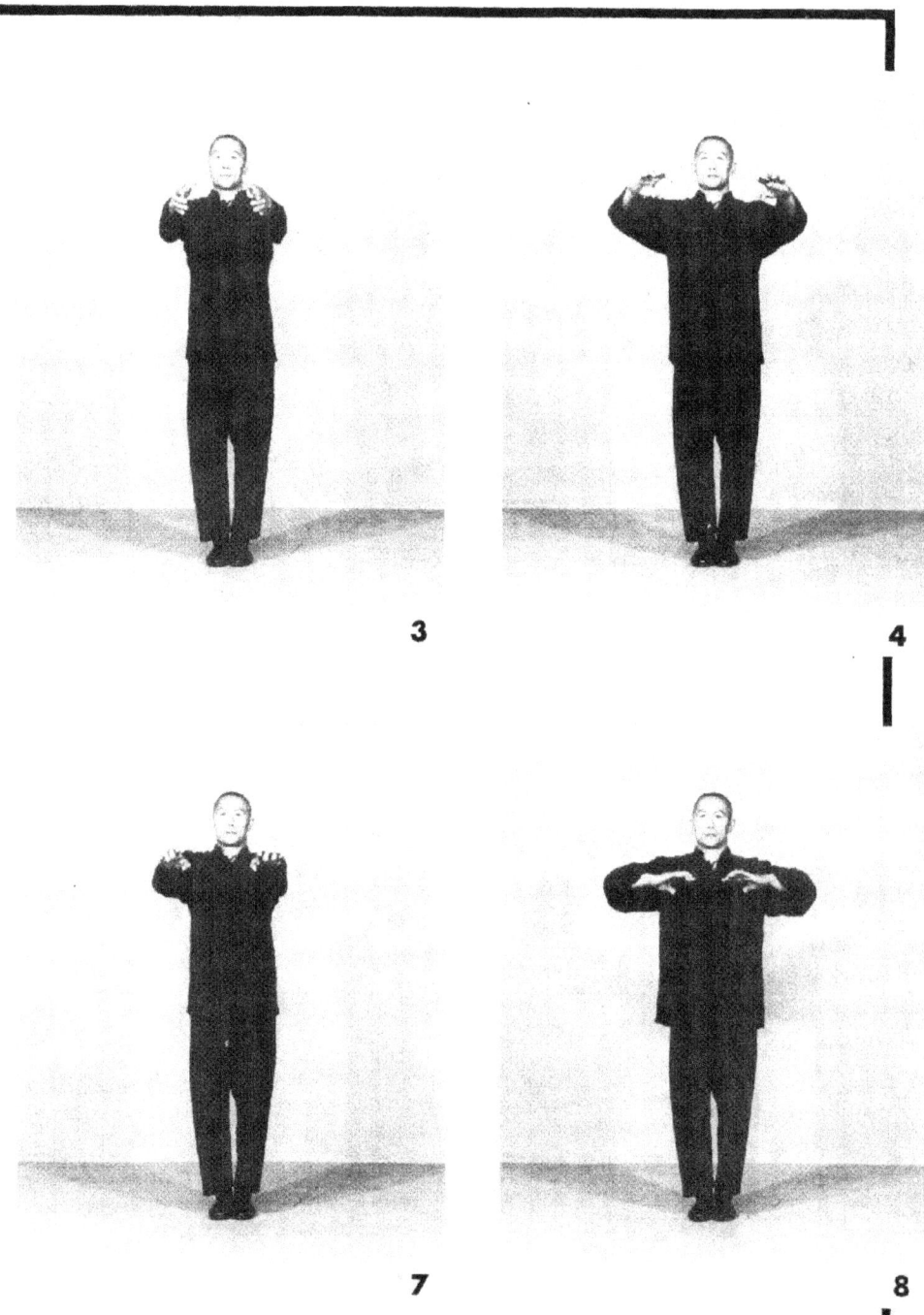

your elbows. (5) Slowly bring your arms to an outstretched position. (6) With palms still facing down, begin to bring your arms inward until (7) your hands are aligned with your shoulders. (8) Move your hands in to your chest.

OPENING THE HORSE (con't)

(9) Slowly rotate your palms counterclockwise, (10) raising your hands until (11) they are above your head, palms facing up. (12) Stretch your hands above your head. (13) Slowly rotate your palms downward to a position

The Chinese Art of Self-Defense

where (14) your fingers are barely touching your shoulders and your elbows are on a horizontal plane. (15) With the backs of your hands facing each other, brush your fingers upward past your ears and (16) above your head.

OPENING THE HORSE (con't)

(17) With your palms facing toward you, lower your hands past your shoulders to waist-level, (18) clenching your fists and bending your knees at the same time. (19) Step to the left with your left foot and (20) assume a horse stance with your weight equally distributed on both legs.

OPEN-HAND BLOCK

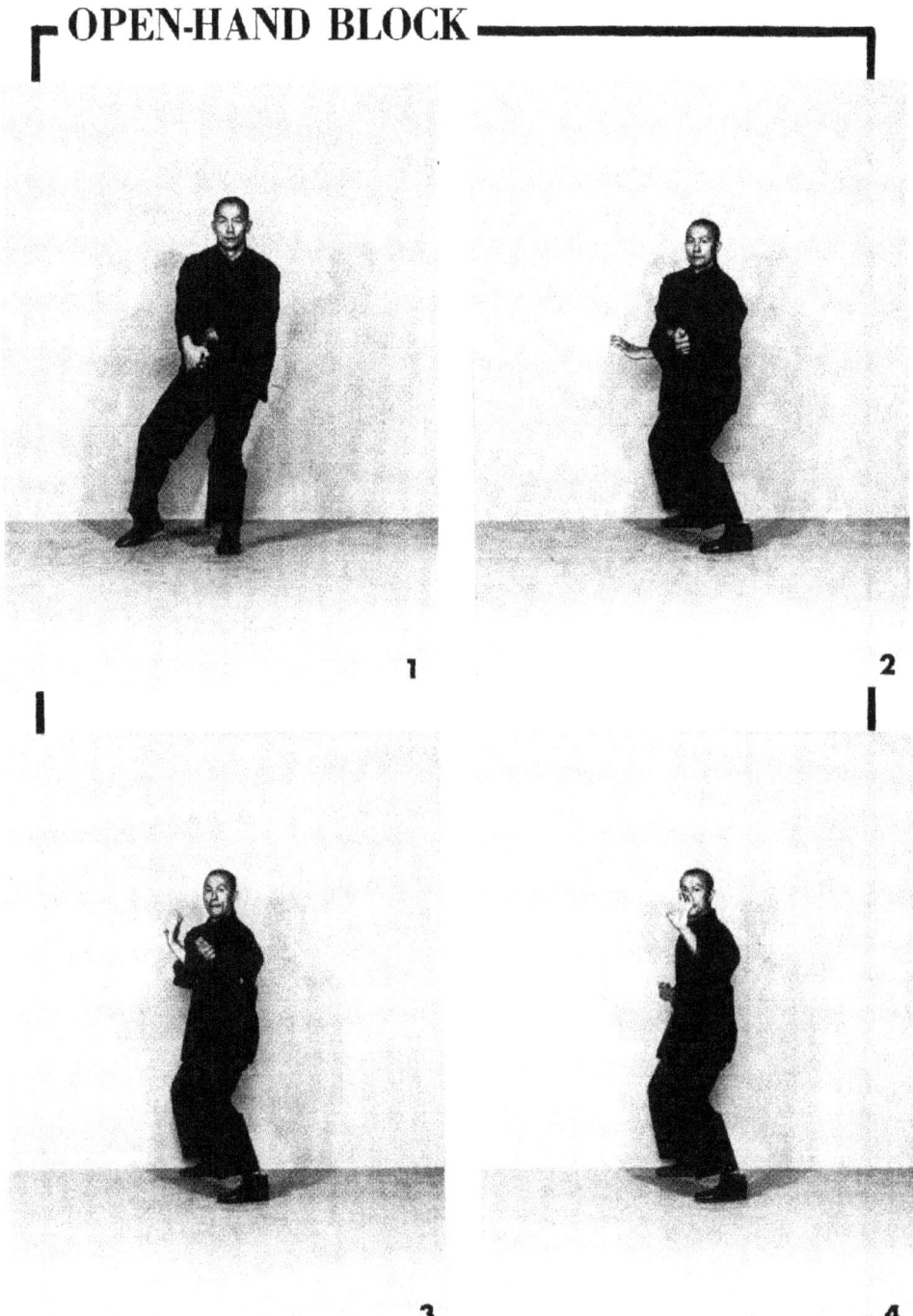

From the horse-stance position, (1) step back on your left foot. (2 & 3) Cross your right hand over your left. (4) Block with your open left hand, simultaneously pulling the right fist back to the lower ribs in a ready position.

CIRCULAR BACK FIST

From the open-hand blocking position, (1) bring your right fist toward your head and lower your open left hand. (2) Pivot to your left and swing your right fist forward in a circular motion. (3) Step forward with your right foot while (4) your right hand circles toward your body. The left hand rises in a protective manner. (5) Continue the circular motion of your right hand, crossing your chest, and (6) deliver the back fist.

1

4

The Chinese Art of Self-Defense

TIGER CLAW

1

2

3

4

From a back-fist position, (1) lower your right fist and (2) raise your open left hand as you step about four inches forward with your left foot into a (3) cat stance and (4) execute a left tiger claw.

SIDE PUNCH

1

2

3

4

(1) From a tiger-claw position, (2) bring your right fist up and (3) shift the right foot forward into a horse stance as you (4) deliver a right side punch.

OPEN-HAND BLOCK and REVERSE PUNCH

1

4

5

From a side-punch position, (1) step forward on your left foot. (2) Cross the right fist over the open left hand. (3 & 4) Bring the right fist back as you apply an open-hand block with your left hand. (5 & 6) Bring your left hand

The Chinese Art of Self-Defense

toward your chest and twist your shoulders into (7) a fully-extended reverse punch.

CIRCULAR GRAB

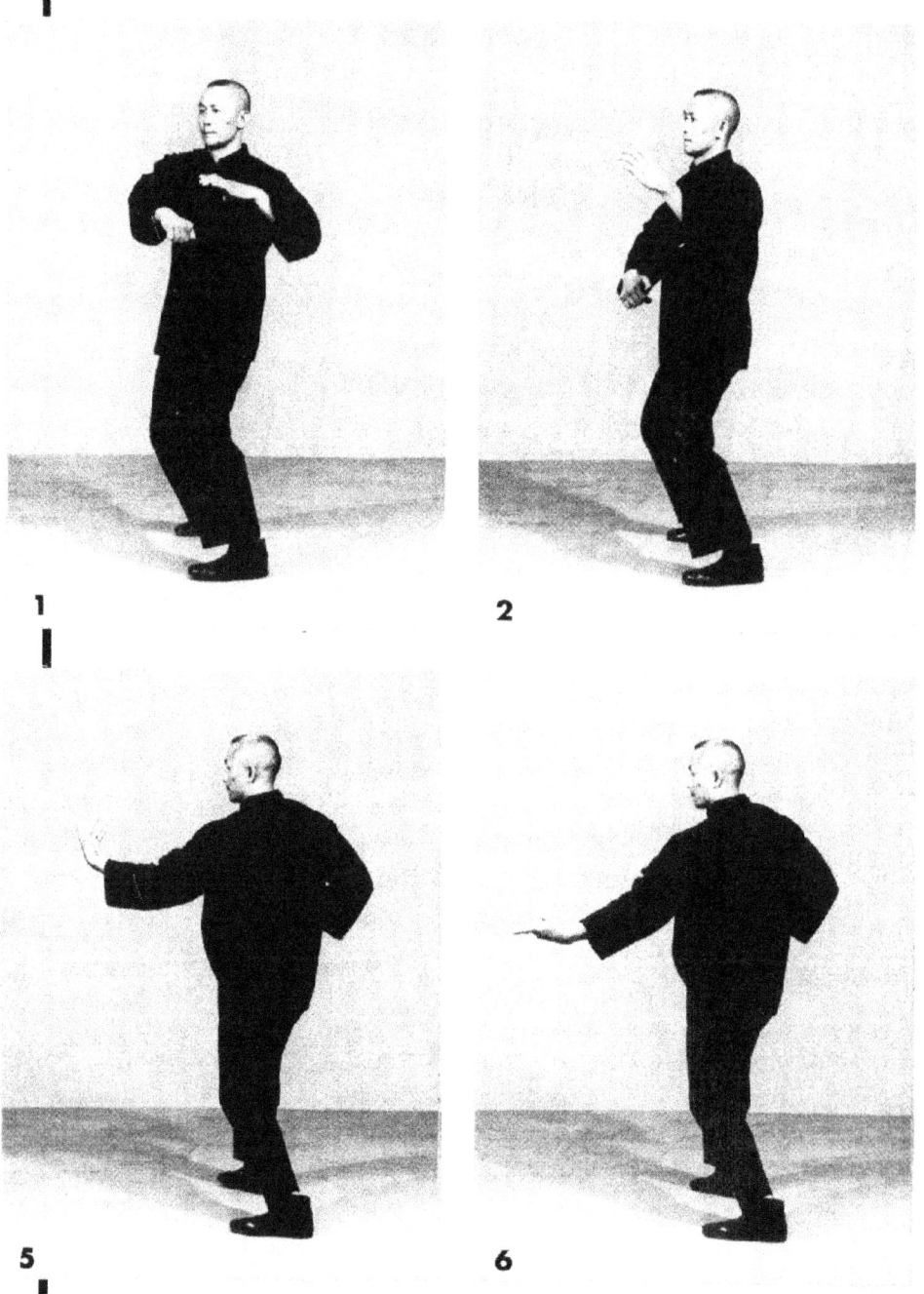

From the reverse-punch position, (1) twist your hips to the right and (2, 3 & 4) bring your open left hand directly in front of your face, with the palm

The Chinese Art of Self-Defense

facing you. (5) Lower your hand as you (6 & 7) circle it clockwise until (8) your arm is almost fully extended to grab with a dragon-head fist.

RIGHT FINGER JAB

From the circular grab position with a dragon-head fist, (1 & 2) simultaneously pivot on the right foot as you circle to the right with your left foot. (3) Draw your left hand to the chest as your right hand—palm up and fingers extended—moves forward to deliver (4) a finger jab.

ELBOW STRIKE

From the finger-jab position, (1) withdraw your right hand to your chest. (2 & 3) With both fists clenched and elbows held horizontally at chest-level, twist your hips to the right and (4) execute an elbow strike.

SIL LUM KUNG-FU

FRONT VIEW

OPEN-HAND BLOCK

In order to better illustrate the movements of the front view (shown at top), Mr. Fong has duplicated them by facing toward the camera in photos 1-8. (1) From the elbow-strike position, (2 & 3) step forward with your left foot into a horse stance, simultaneously crossing your left hand under your right. (4 &

The Chinese Art of Self-Defense

and REVERSE PUNCH

5) Execute an open-hand block and prepare for a reverse punch by (6) lowering your open left hand to the chest for protective measures. (7 & 8) Apply the reverse punch.

INSIDE MIDDLE BLOCK and FINGER JAB

(1) From the reverse-punch position, (2) pivot on your right foot and step back with the left. (3) With the fist clenched, bring your right arm up to eye-level. (4) Twist your elbow to the left and with the left side of your forearm deliver an inside middle block. (5) Retract your right arm as you simultaneously (6) deliver a finger jab with the left hand.

The Chinese Art of Self-Defense

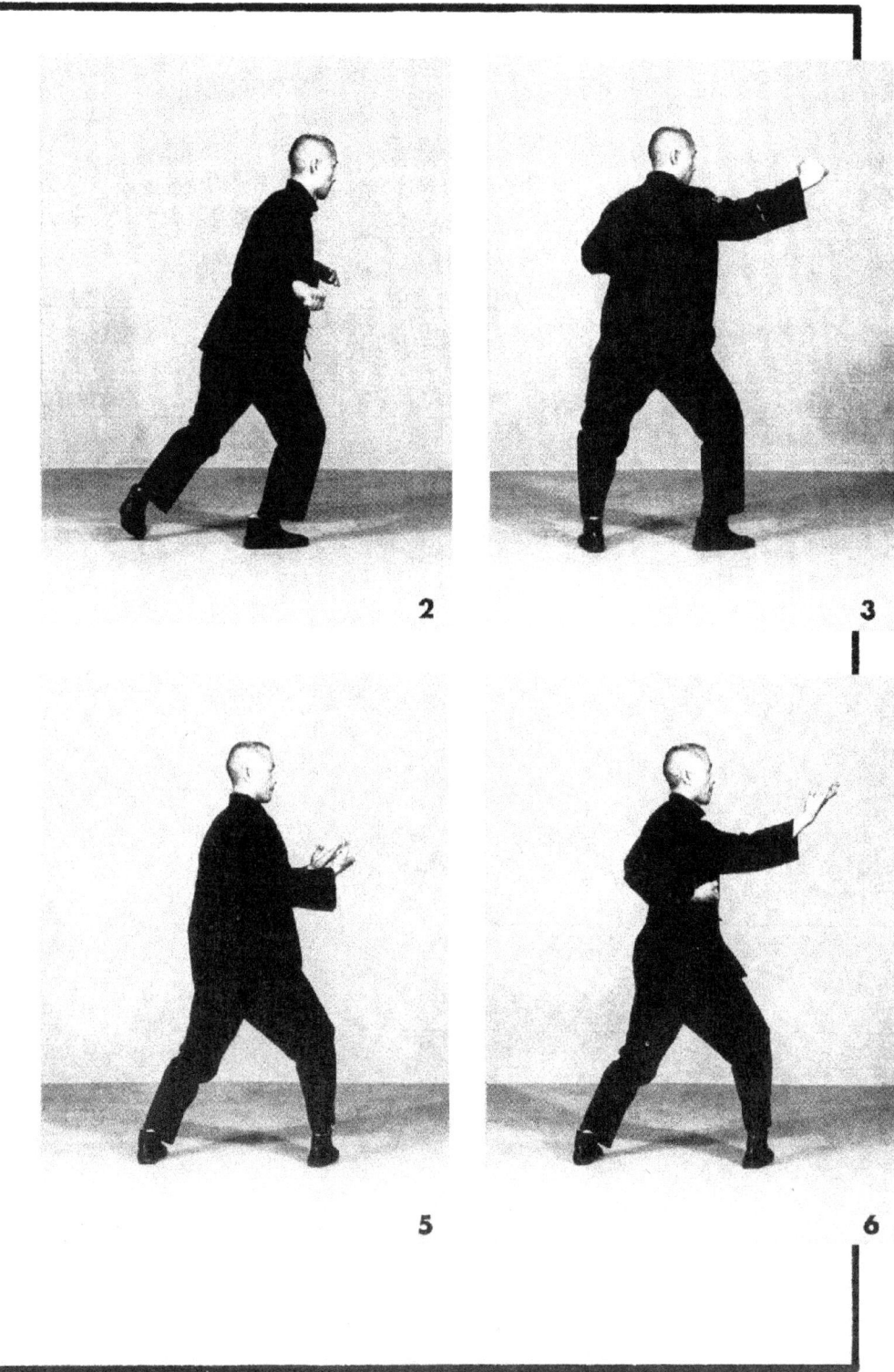

HAMMER FIST STRIKE

From the finger-jab position, (1) begin to retract your open left hand as you move into a (2) horse stance—your left arm across your chest and your right fist below your left elbow. (3) Begin to swing your right fist to the right in order to (4) deliver a hammer fist strike.

DOUBLE FIST STRIKE

From the hammer-fist position, (1) pivot slightly on your left foot and (2) step back with the right foot as you lift both fists behind your head. (3) Simultaneously swing both fists forward and (4) execute a double fist strike at chest-level.

OPEN-HAND BLOCK

1

2

3

4

From the double fist strike position, (1) move the open left hand to a position beneath the right arm as you step back with your left foot. (2) Align your feet by stepping back with your right foot, and (3) assume a horse stance, (4) simultaneously drawing the right fist back to your hip and extending the open left hand forward to execute an open-hand block.

CANNON PUNCH

From the open-hand block position, (1) pivot on the left foot, (2) raising your right fist high as you (3) step forward with the right foot and, at the same time, rotating your arm as if pitching underhanded to (4) execute an uppercut-like cannon punch.

CIRCULAR BLOCK and FINGER JAB

(1) From the cannon-punch position, (2) begin the circular block by (3) rotating both of your open hands in a clockwise motion to the left as you (4) cross your left foot over your right. (5) Align your right foot (6) just before you thrust a finger jab.

1

4

The Chinese Art of Self-Defense

OPEN-HAND BLOCK and REVERSE PUNCH

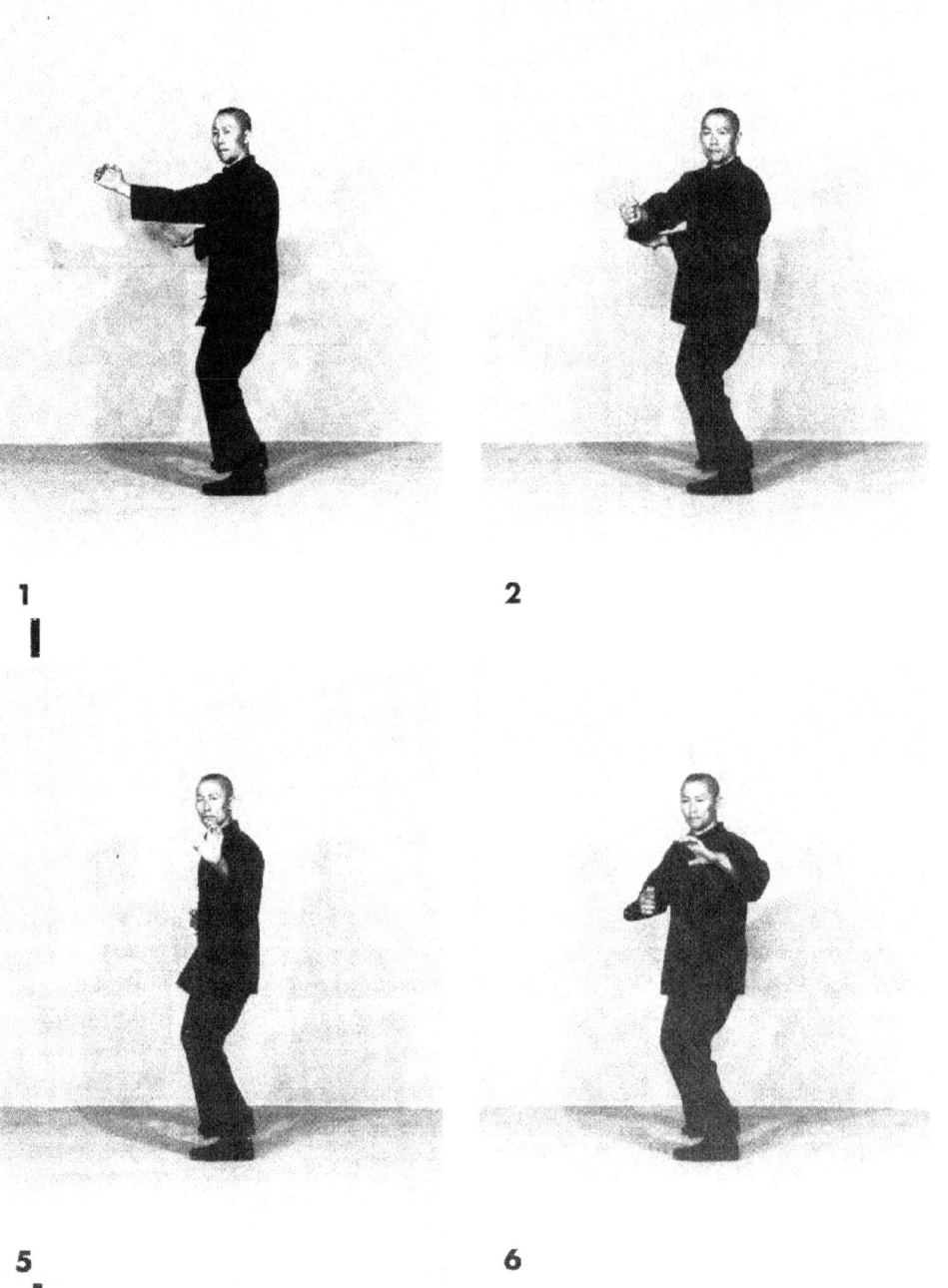

From the circular block position, (1) remain in a horse stance as you face in the opposite direction. (2 & 3) Cross your right hand over your left, (4) extending your left hand to block as you (5) pull your right hand to your

The Chinese Art of Self-Defense

right hip. (6) Begin the reverse punch by (7) drawing your open left hand back to your chest as a protective measure. (8) Execute a right reverse punch.

INWARD BLOCK and LEFT FINGER JAB

(1) From the right reverse punch position, (2 & 3) step forward on your right foot in a 90-degree body turn and (4) snap your right elbow in an inward block, (5 & 6) simultaneously retracting your right hand to your hip and executing a left finger jab.

1

4

The Chinese Art of Self-Defense

SIL LUM KUNG-FU

SLICE BLOCK, REVERSE PUNCH and

From a left finger jab position, (1) retract your left hand, (2) facing your body forward in a 90-degree body turn. (3) Keep your right hand close to your body as you slice block with the left hand. (4) Deliver a reverse punch

The Chinese Art of Self-Defense

SLICE BLOCK

with the right hand. (5 & 6) Simultaneously step back on your right foot and return your right hand (palm up) to your hip. (7 & 8) Your left hand remains in a slice-block position as a protective measure.

RIDGE-HAND and TIGER CLAW

(1) From a slice-block position, (2 & 3) simultaneously raise your right hand toward your face and step forward with your right foot. (4) Level your right arm in a ridge-hand position. (5) Raising your left hand, take a half-step forward with your left foot and (6) execute a tiger claw. Most of your weight should be placed on your left leg.

1

4

The Chinese Art of Self-Defense

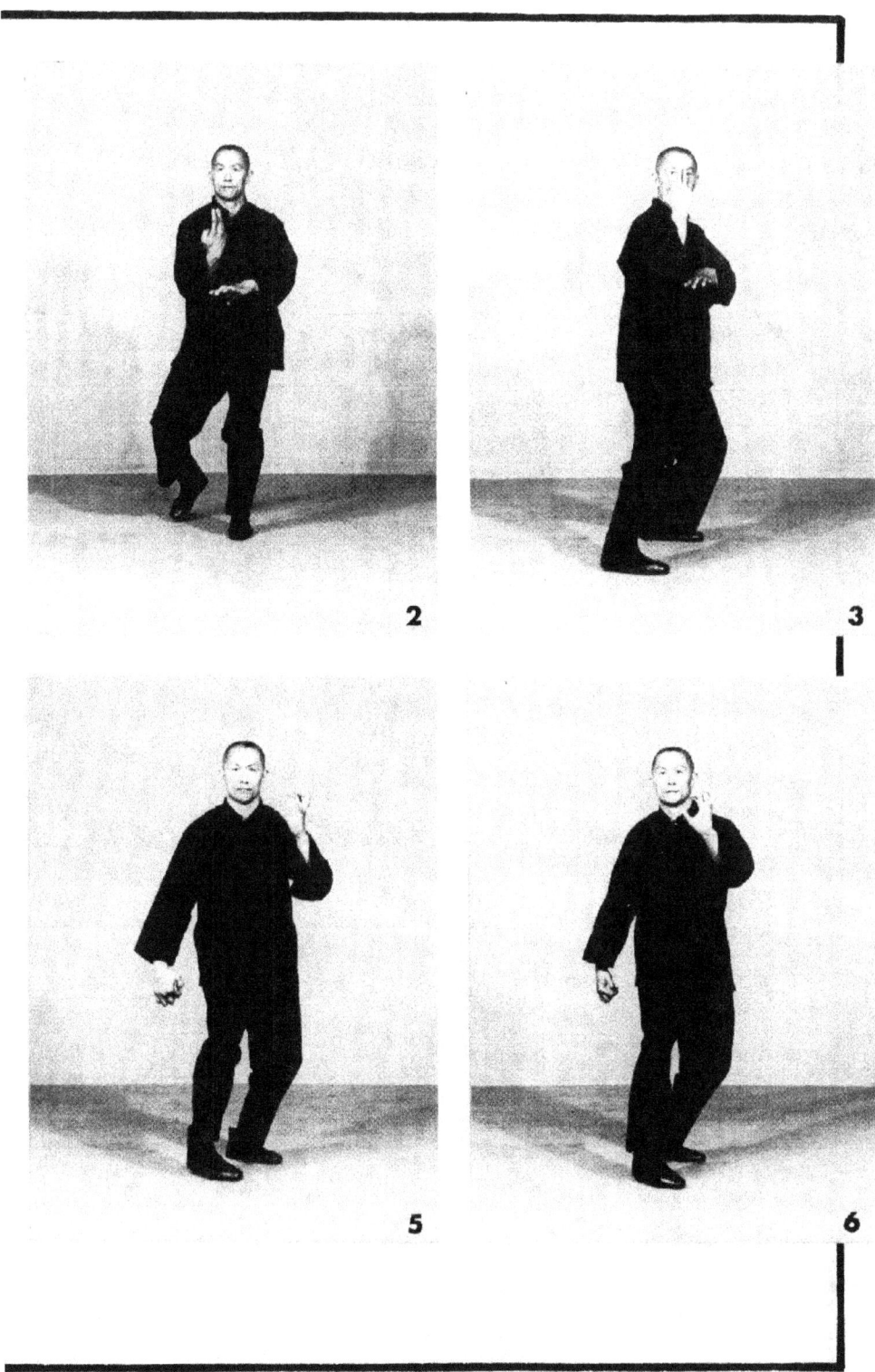

CANNON PUNCH, CIRCULAR BLOCK and

From the tiger-claw position, (1) retract your left hand to your chest as you return to a horse stance. (2) Swing your right hand up to (3) execute an uppercut cannon punch. (4, 5 & 6) Begin to cross you left foot over your

FINGER JAB

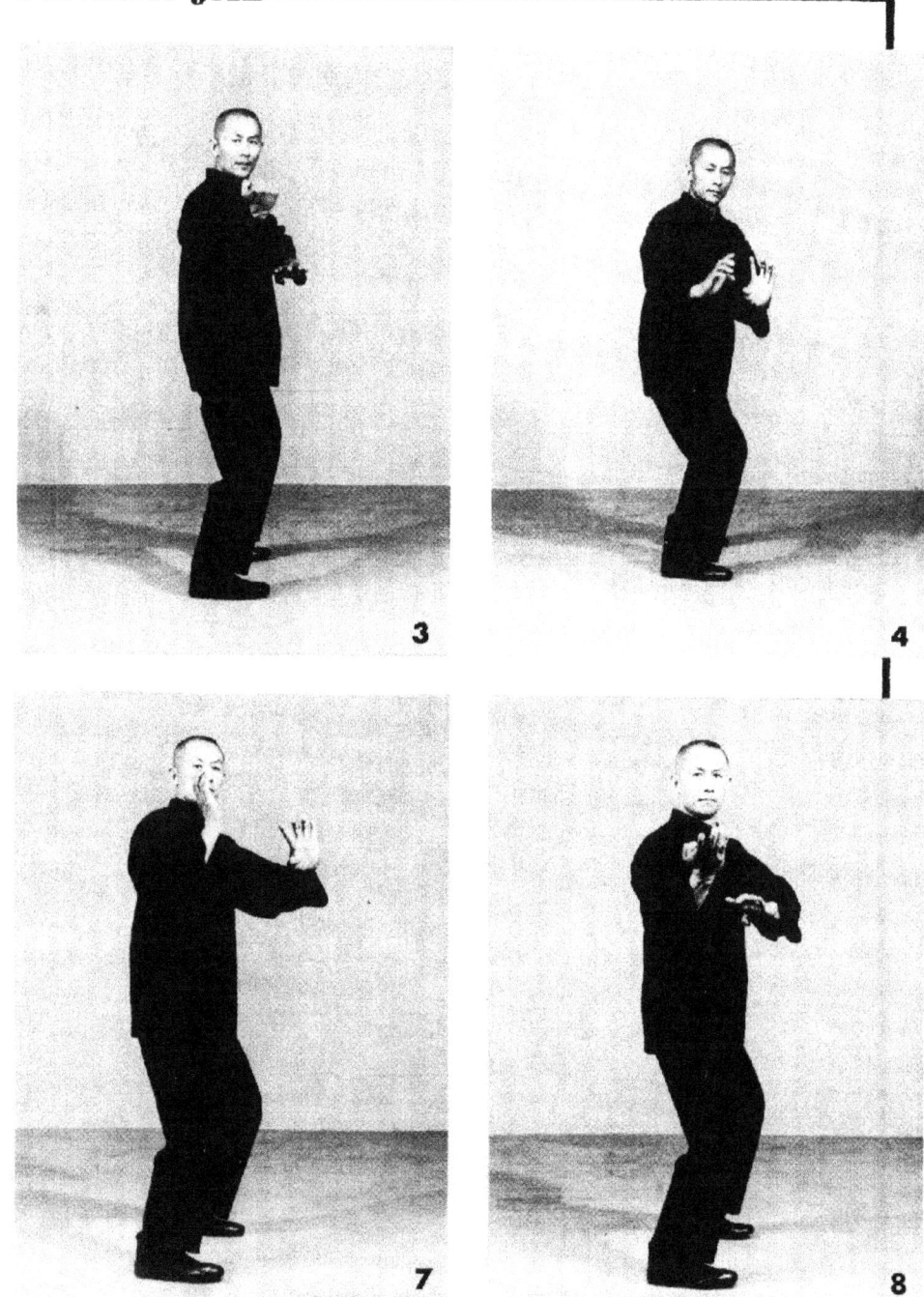

right as you rotate your hands clockwise in a circular block. (7) Step off with the right foot as you (8) thrust the right hand into a finger jab. Your left hand should remain across your chest as a protective measure.

OPEN-HAND BLOCK

(1) From the right finger jab position, (2 & 3) turn to your left on the opposite side and simultaneously retract your right hand, (4) crossing it over the left to (5) execute a left, open-hand block. (6) Bring your right fist to your hip.

The Chinese Art of Self-Defense

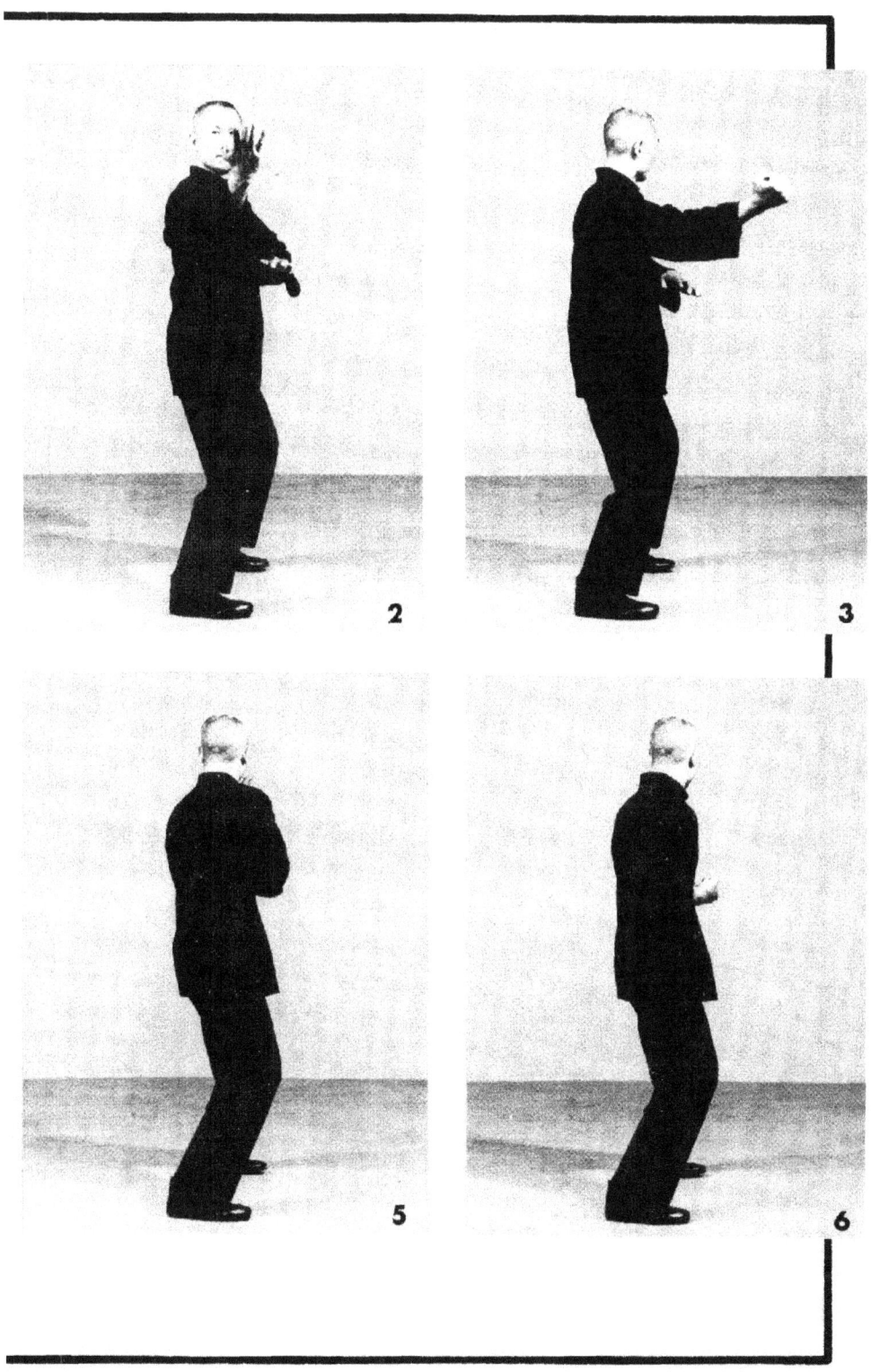

INWARD BLOCK and FINGER JAB

From the open-hand block position, (1 & 2) step forward 90 degrees with the right foot, returning your left hand to your chest and, at the same time, (3 & 4) snapping your elbow for an inward block. (5) Return your right hand to your hip and (6) thrust your left hand into a finger jab.

The Chinese Art of Self-Defense

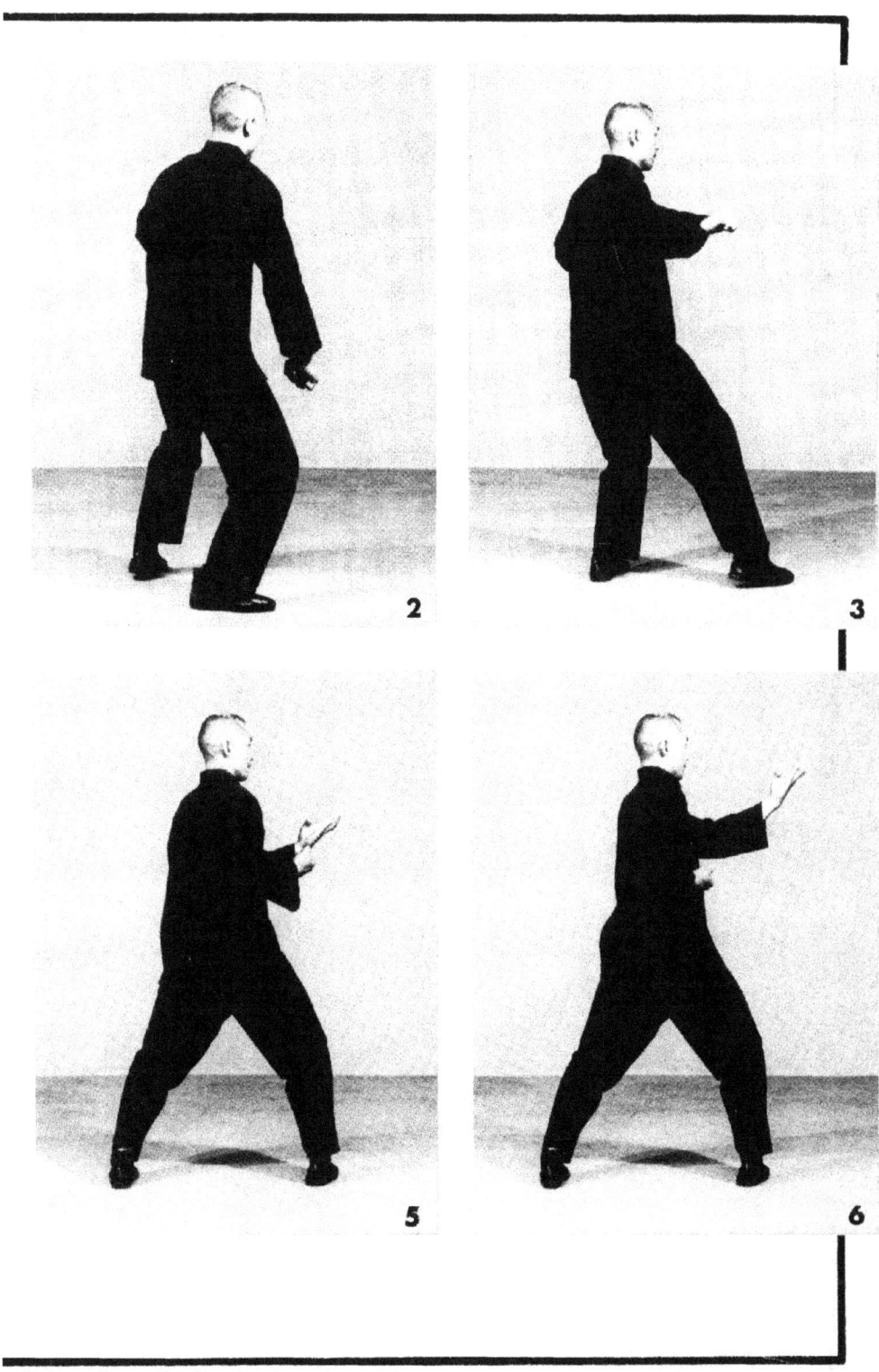

SLICE BLOCK and REVERSE PUNCH

1

2

3

The Chinese Art of Self-Defense

FRONT VIEW

In order to better illustrate the movements of the front view (shown above), Mr. Fong has duplicated them by facing toward the camera in photos 1-5. (1) From the left finger jab position, (2) twist the upper part of your body to the front, returning your open left hand, palm down, to your body. (3 & 4) Begin a slice block with your left hand and (5) execute a reverse punch.

4

5

SIL LUM KUNG-FU

FRONT VIEW

SLICE BLOCK
and
RIDGE-HAND
ATTACK

1

2

3

The Chinese Art of Self-Defense

In order to better illustrate the movements of the front view (shown above), Mr. Fong has duplicated them by facing toward the camera in photos 1-5. From the reverse-punch position, (1) withdraw your right hand to your body. (2) Step forward with the left foot into a side horse stance, placing your open left hand over your right fist. (3) Pivot your left foot so your toes point forward, and simultaneously execute a slice block. (4) Step forward with your right foot as you bring your right hand up, fingers extended. (5) Pivot to your left into a horse stance, and execute a ridge-hand attack.

4

5

FRONT VIEW

TIGER CLAW
and
CANNON PUNCH

1

2

3

The Chinese Art of Self-Defense

In order to better illustrate the movements of the front view (shown above), Mr. Fong has duplicated them by facing toward the camera in photos 1-5. From the ridge-hand attack position, (1) move your left foot slightly toward the right, (2) shifting most of your weight to the rear foot. Execute a tiger claw. (3) Turn your right toes to the left and assume a horse stance as you (4) return your open left hand to your chest for protective measures. (5) Execute a cannon punch.

4

5

SIL LUM KUNG-FU

FRONT VIEW

CIRCULAR BLOCK
and
RIGHT FINGER JAB

1

2

3

The Chinese Art of Self-Defense

In order to better illustrate the movements of the front view (shown above), Mr. Fong has duplicated them by facing toward the camera in photos 1-5. From the cannon punch position, (1 & 2) cross your left leg over your right as you begin rotating your hands in a clockwise movement, and (3) deliver a circular block. (4) Step off with your right foot into a horse stance as you (5) execute a finger jab, placing your left hand across your chest for protective measures.

OPEN-HAND BLOCK and REVERSE PUNCH-

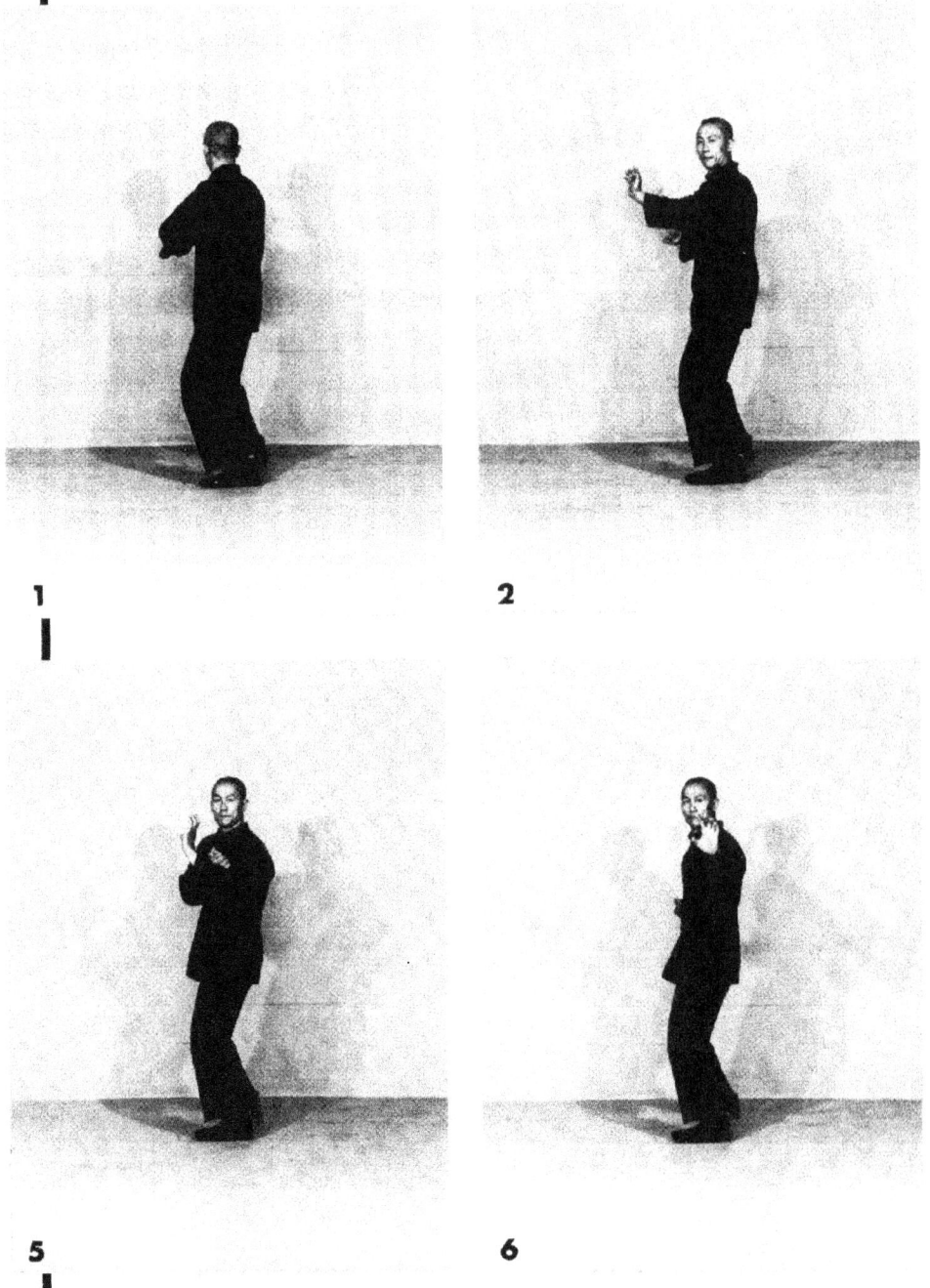

(1) From a right finger jab position, (2) turn to your left in the opposite direction, (3 & 4) simultaneously crossing your right hand over your left. (5 & 6) Raising your left open hand in a blocking position, retract your right fist

The Chinese Art of Self-Defense

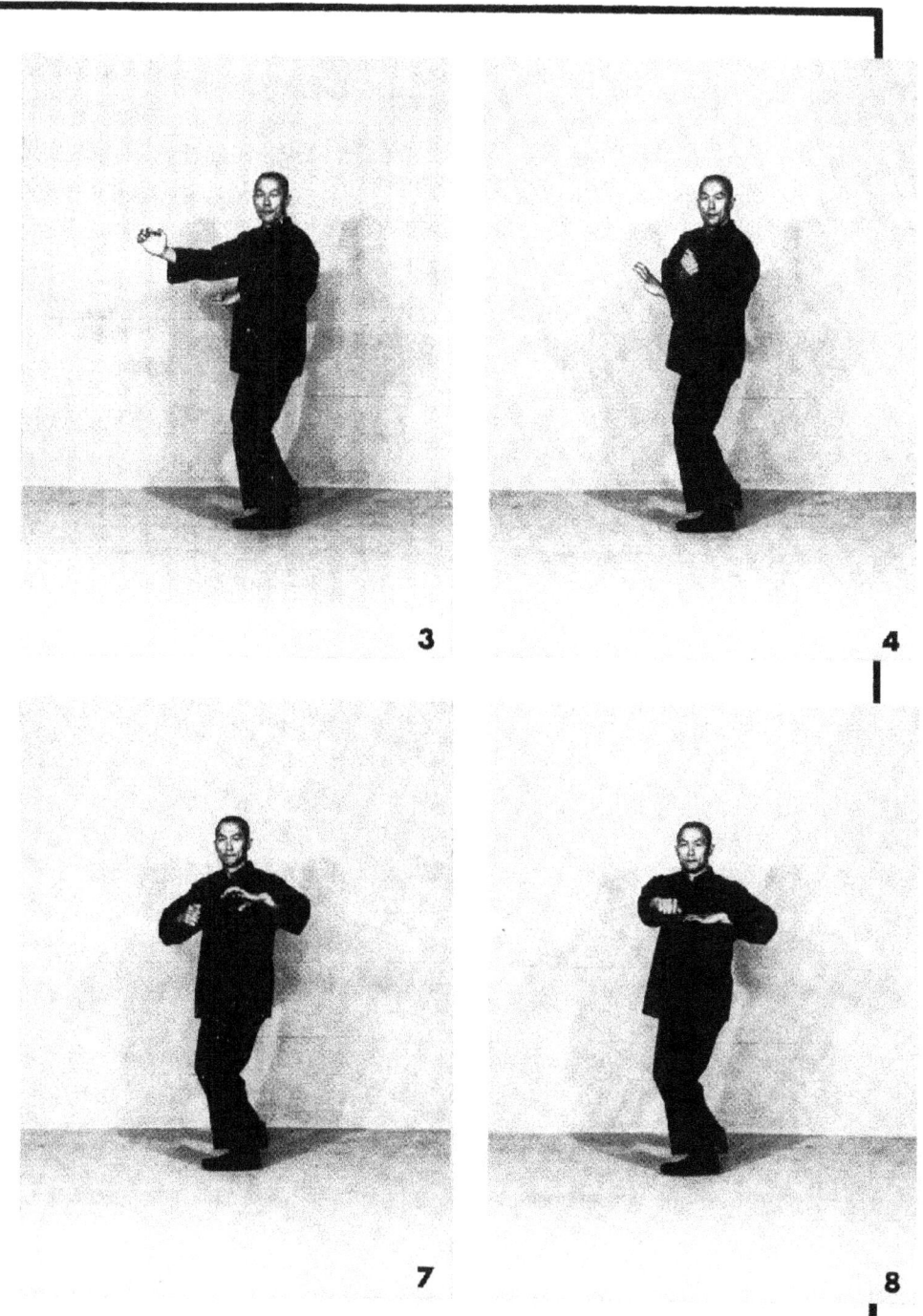

to your hip. (7 & 8) As a protective measure, return your left open hand (palm down) to your chest and twist the upper part of your body to execute a reverse punch.

SHIFTING LEFT OPEN-HAND BLOCK and

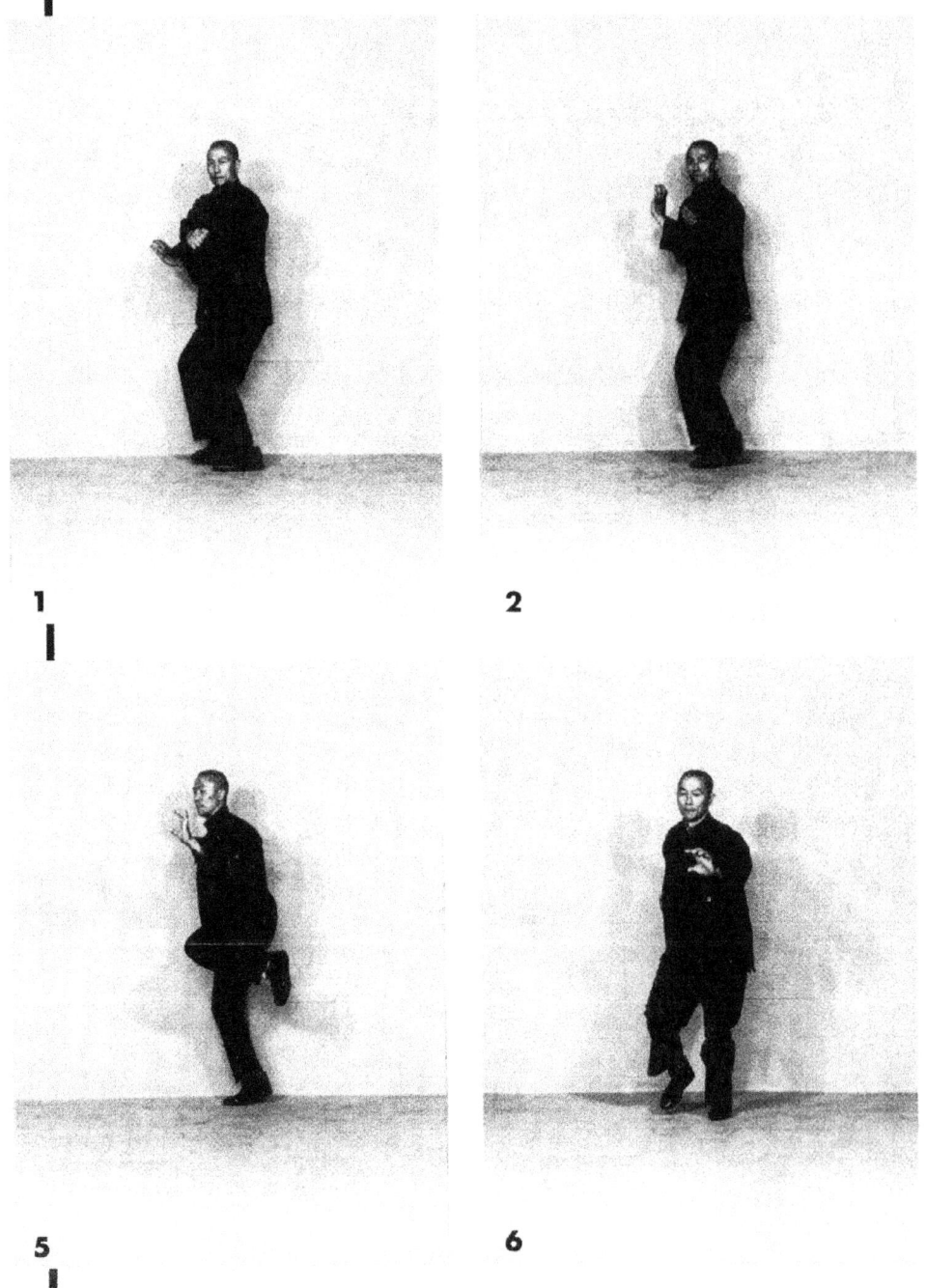

From the reverse-punch position, (1 & 2) return to a horse stance, arms crossed. (3) Retract your right fist to your hip and block with your open left hand. (4, 5, 6 & 7) Leap 180 degrees to the left, your body faced in the

STRAIGHT SIDE CANNON PUNCH

opposite direction. (8) Retract your left hand to your chest as a protective measure while executing the straight lunge cannon punch.

CIRCULAR BACK FIST and SINGLE

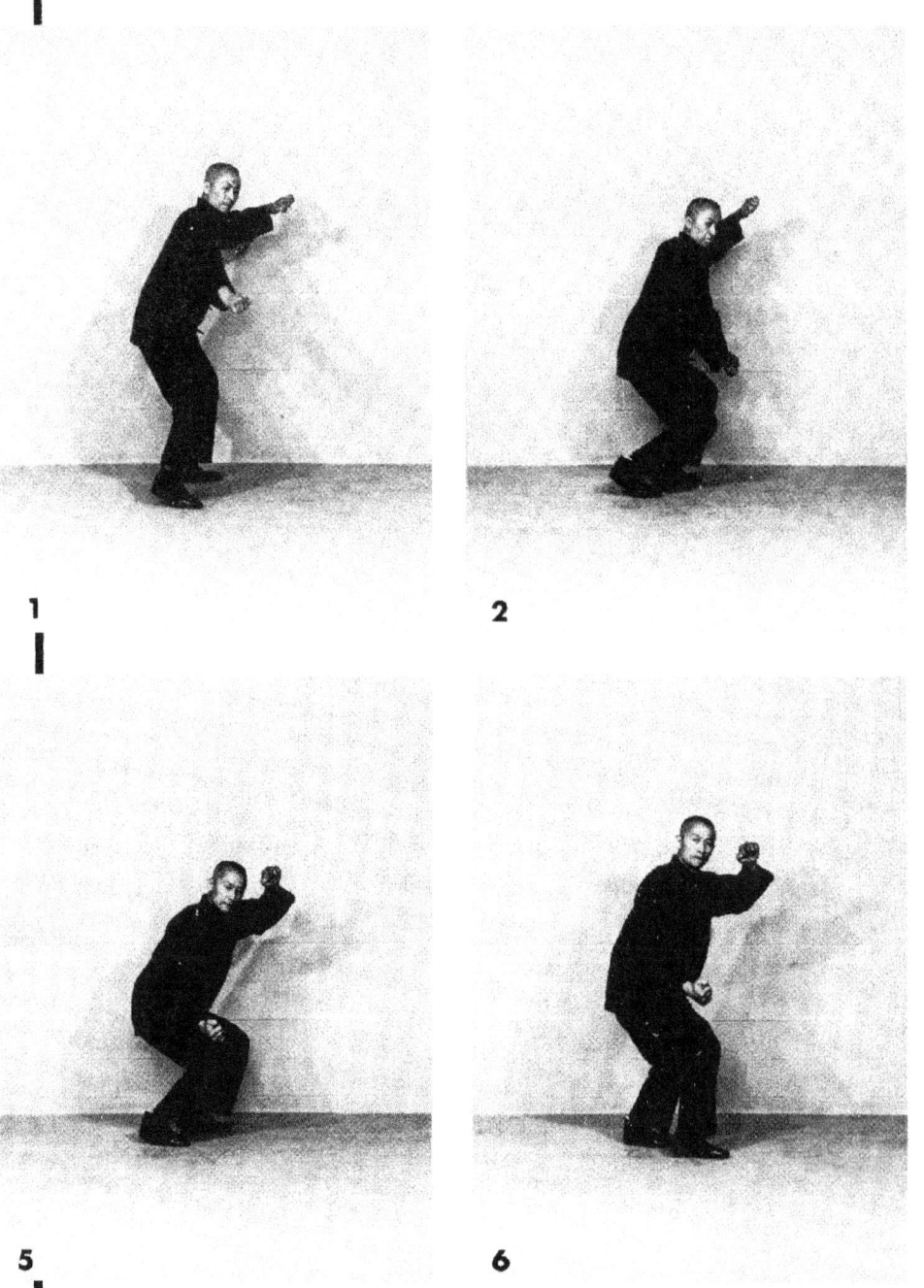

From the cannon punch position, (1) bend down into a very low horse stance, (2) your left hand clenched near your head for protection. (3 & 4) Rotate your right hand in a circular back fist strike. (5 & 6) Raise your body

FLYING-FOOT KICK

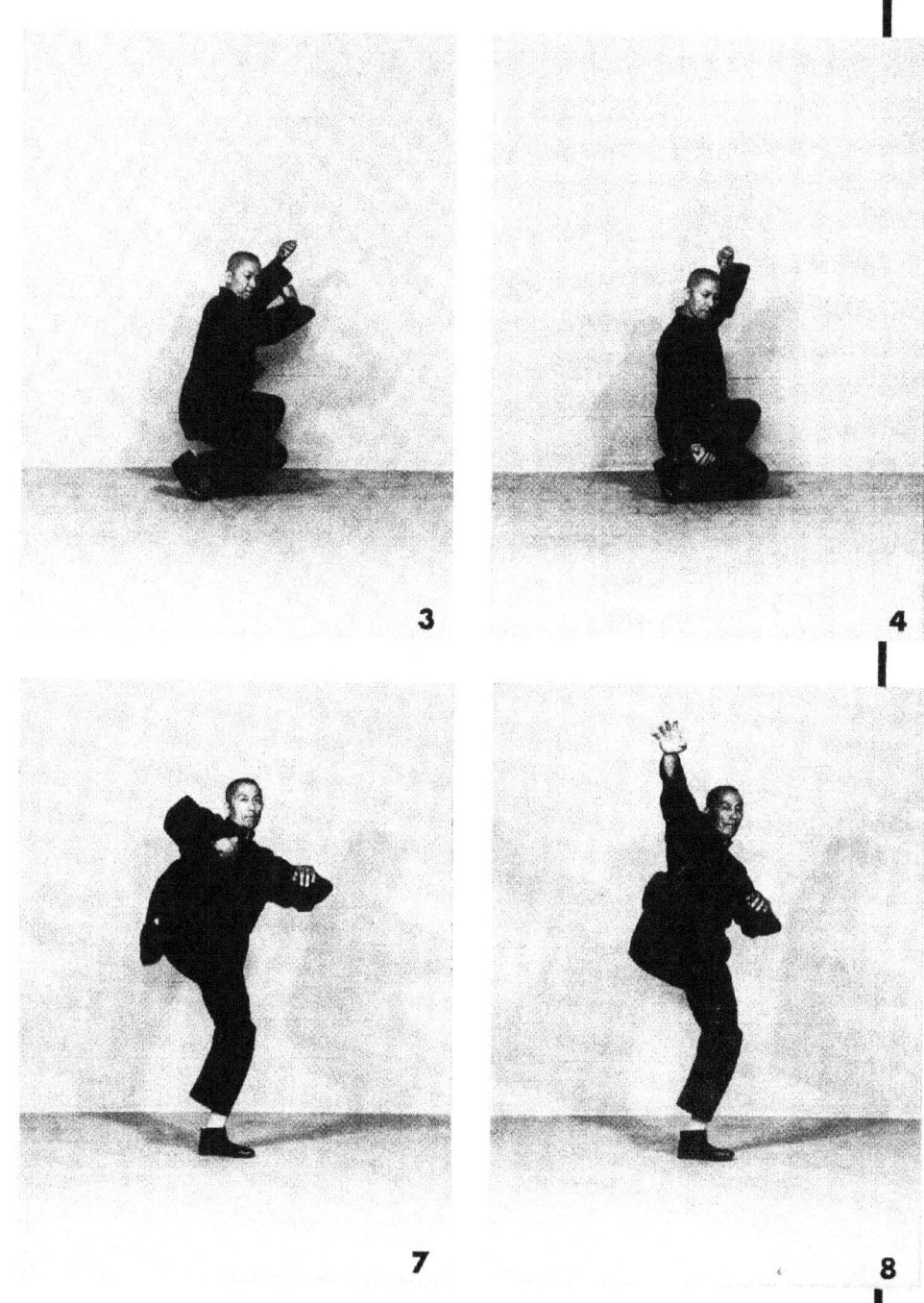

slightly and cross your left leg over your right, (7 & 8) simultaneously snapping both a high backhand strike and a right kick.

CLOSING THE FORM

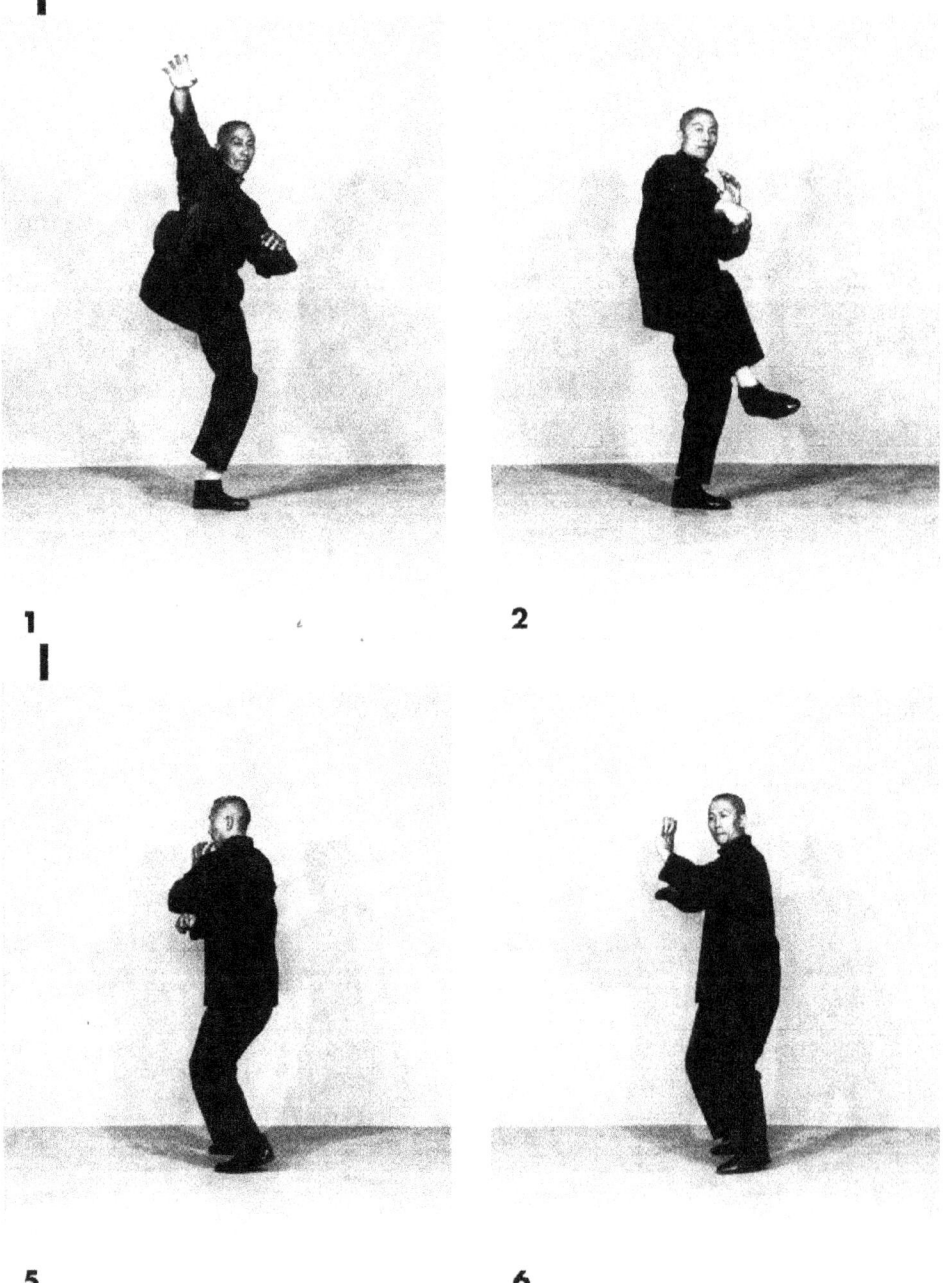

(1) From the single flying-foot kick position, (2) cross your right foot over your left and (3) your right hand under your left. (4 & 5) Pivot in the opposite direction (180 degrees) by stepping off with the left foot into a cat stance, and (6) simultaneously bring your left hand into an open block

The Chinese Art of Self-Defense

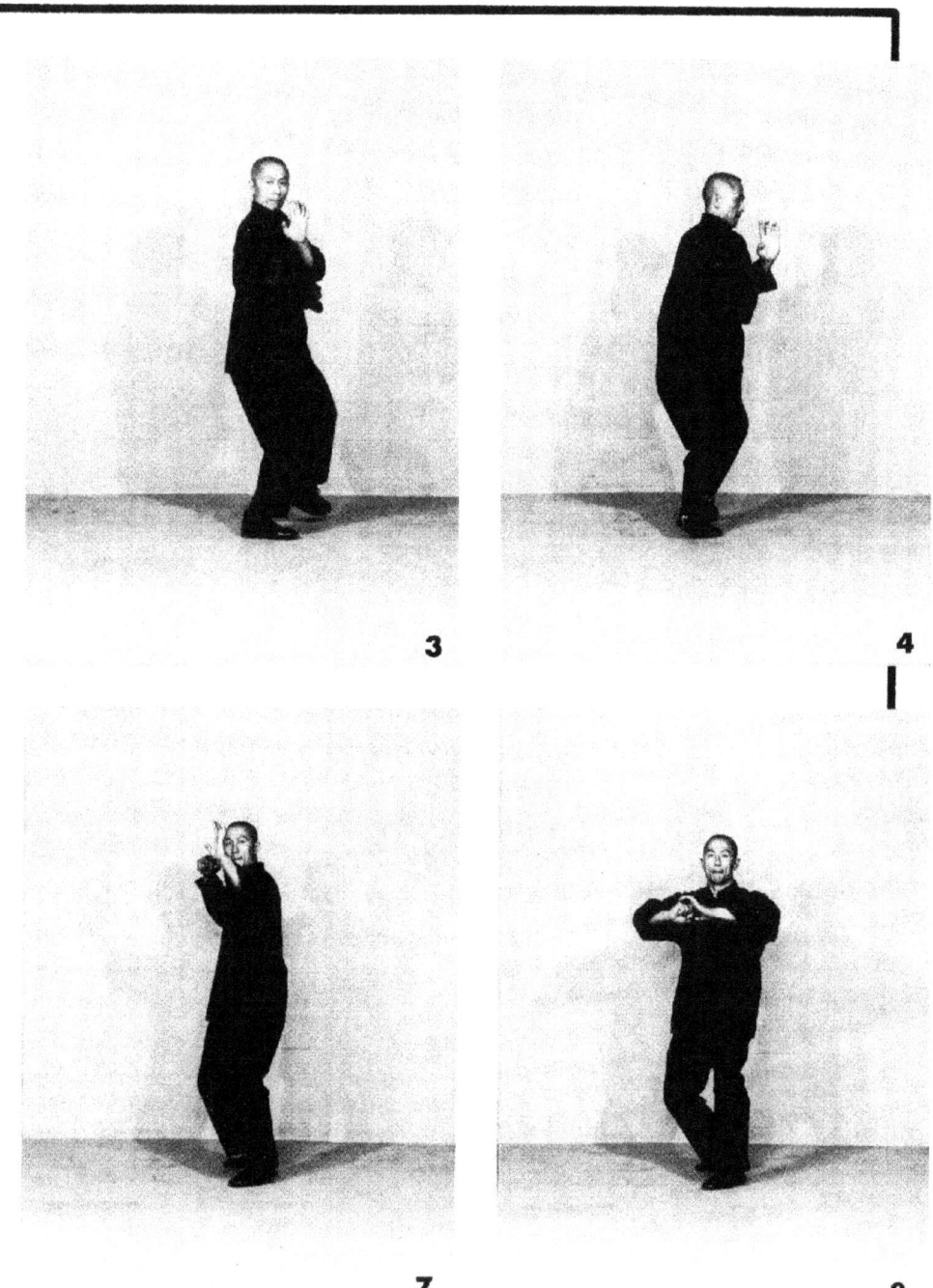

position. (7) Raise your right fist to a horizontal position with your elbow parallel to your shoulder. (8 & 9) Pivot slightly to the left on your right foot and lower both hands—the left hand over the right fist in a cover position. Then thrust your hands slightly forward. (10) Place your right foot in line

CLOSING THE FORM (cont)

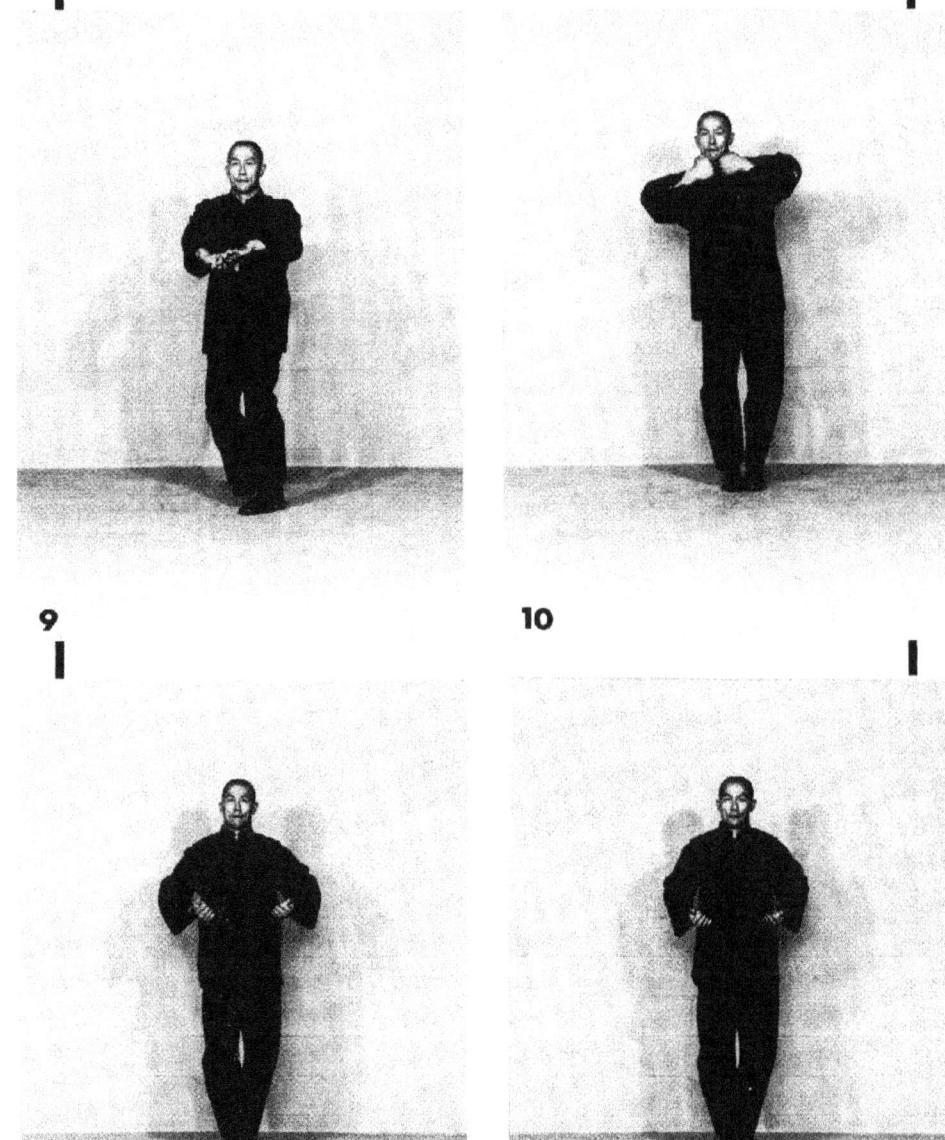

with the left and simultaneously raise both fists—clenched and facing each other—to your chin. (11) Making a wide, forward arc, (12) return your hands to waist-level.

LIN WAN KUNE COMPLETE

The following pages are an uninterrupted, overall view of Lin Wan Kune, illustrating the continuity and flow of its form.

LIN WAN KUNE COMPLETE

The Continuous and Returning Fist

OPENING THE HORSE

OPENING THE HORSE (Con't.)

OPENING THE HORSE (Con't.)

OPENING THE HORSE (Con't.)

The Chinese Art of Self-Defense

SIL LUM KUNG-FU

TIGER CLAW

SIDE PUNCH

REVERSE PUNCH

The Chinese Art of Self-Defense

OPEN-HAND BLOCK

CIRCULAR BACK FIST

The Chinese Art of Self-Defense

FINGER JAB

MIDDLE BLOCK

HAMMER FIST

DOUBLE FIST STRIKE

CANNON PUNCH

CIRCULAR BLOCK

REVERSE PUNCH

The Chinese Art of Self-Defense

SIL LUM KUNG-FU

SLICE BLOCK   REVERSE PUNCH

SLICE BLOCK   RIDGE HAND

CANNON PUNCH

The Chinese Art of Self-Defense

TIGER CLAW

CIRCULAR BLOCK FINGER JAB

PEN-HAND BLOCK

SIL LUM KUNG-FU

INWARD BLOCK · FINGER JAB · SLICE BLOCK

SLICE BLOCK

CANNON PUNCH

The Chinese Art of Self-Defense

REVERSE PUNCH

TIGER CLAW

CIRCULAR BLOCK   FINGER JAB

OPEN-HAND BLOCK

REVERSE PUNCH

CANNON PUNCH

CIRCULAR BACK FIST

The Chinese Art of Self-Defense

OPEN-HAND BLOCK

INGLE FLYING FOOT

CLOSING THE FORM

APPLICATION OF FORM

One of the ultimate goals of Kung-Fu practice is the ability to apply the art to combat, in a life and death situation. This section on breakdown attempts to prepare the Kung-Fu student for the application of theory in practice. The form practice in the previous section is valuable in orienting the Kung-Fu practitioner to the movements of application. Repetition is of vital importance in developing the physical and mental aspect of free fighting. All movements must be smooth, fluid and simultaneous. Most important is the ability to concentrate and use the imagination during the execution of all movements.

Right Punch Defense

(1) Stand in a ready position with your left foot forward. (2) Wait for your opponent to make the first move. (3) As he lunges forward with a right punch, throw a finger jab to his eyes, automatically blocking his blow. (4) As soon as you have blocked, keep your body balanced as you prepare to

counter with a reverse punch to his body. (5) When he blocks your punch, (6) leave your left hand at chest level to protect yourself from his counter while you bring your right hand up to counter. (7) Quickly counter with a backhand. (8) Apply your punch directly to his temple, keeping your right foot close to his left foot to prevent him from kicking.

Lunge Punch Trap Defense

(1) Stand in a ready position with both hands up and your left foot forward. (2) Prepare to avoid your opponent's punch. (3) The instant he makes his move, quickly shift your body to the left, ducking the blow. (4) Then move into him with your right

The Chinese Art of Self-Defense

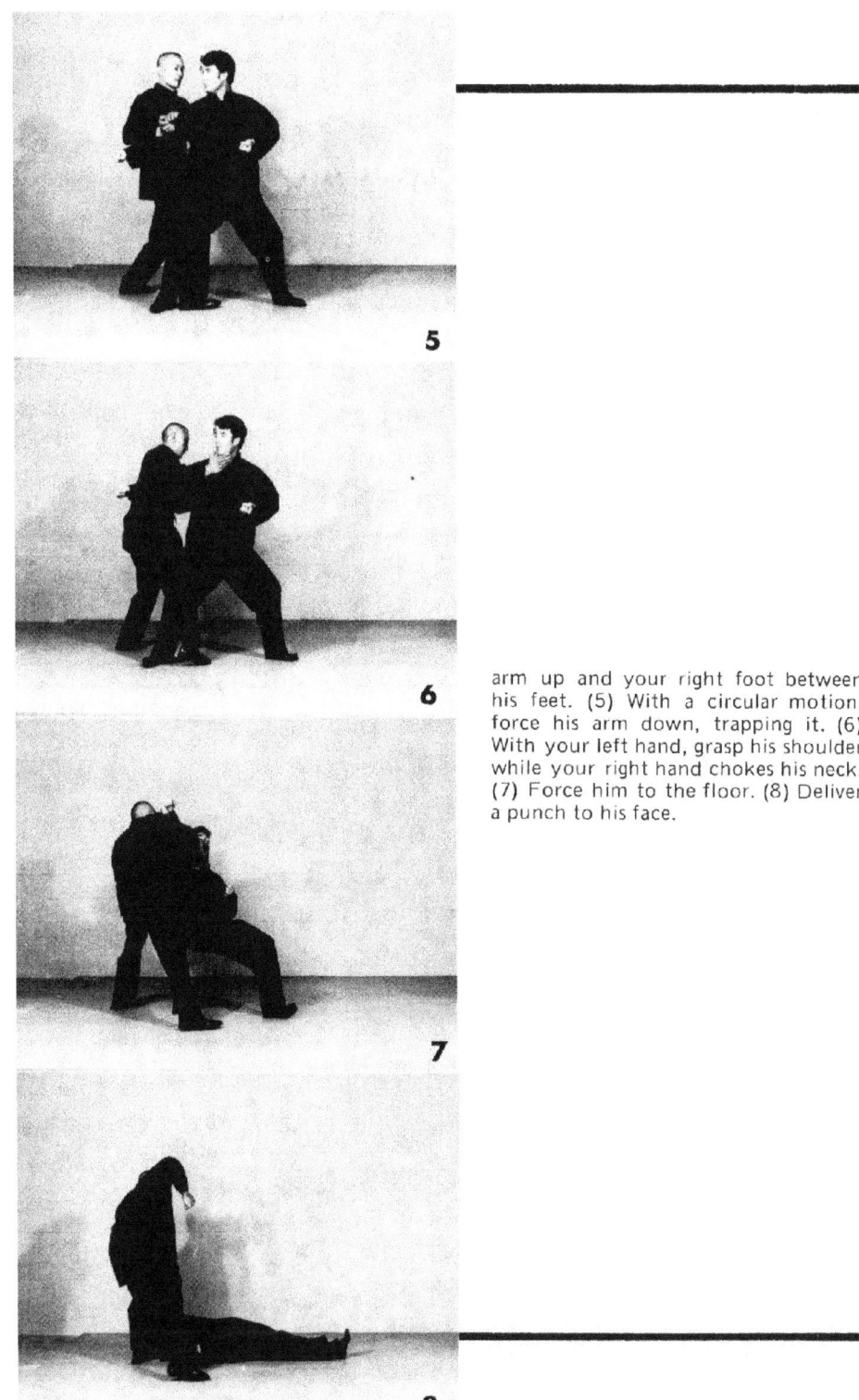

arm up and your right foot between his feet. (5) With a circular motion, force his arm down, trapping it. (6) With your left hand, grasp his shoulder while your right hand chokes his neck. (7) Force him to the floor. (8) Deliver a punch to his face.

Left Jab Defense

(1) Stand in a ready position with both hands up and your left foot forward. (2) As your opponent jabs with his left hand, block with your left and (3) quickly grab his arm. (4) Turn

The Chinese Art of Self-Defense

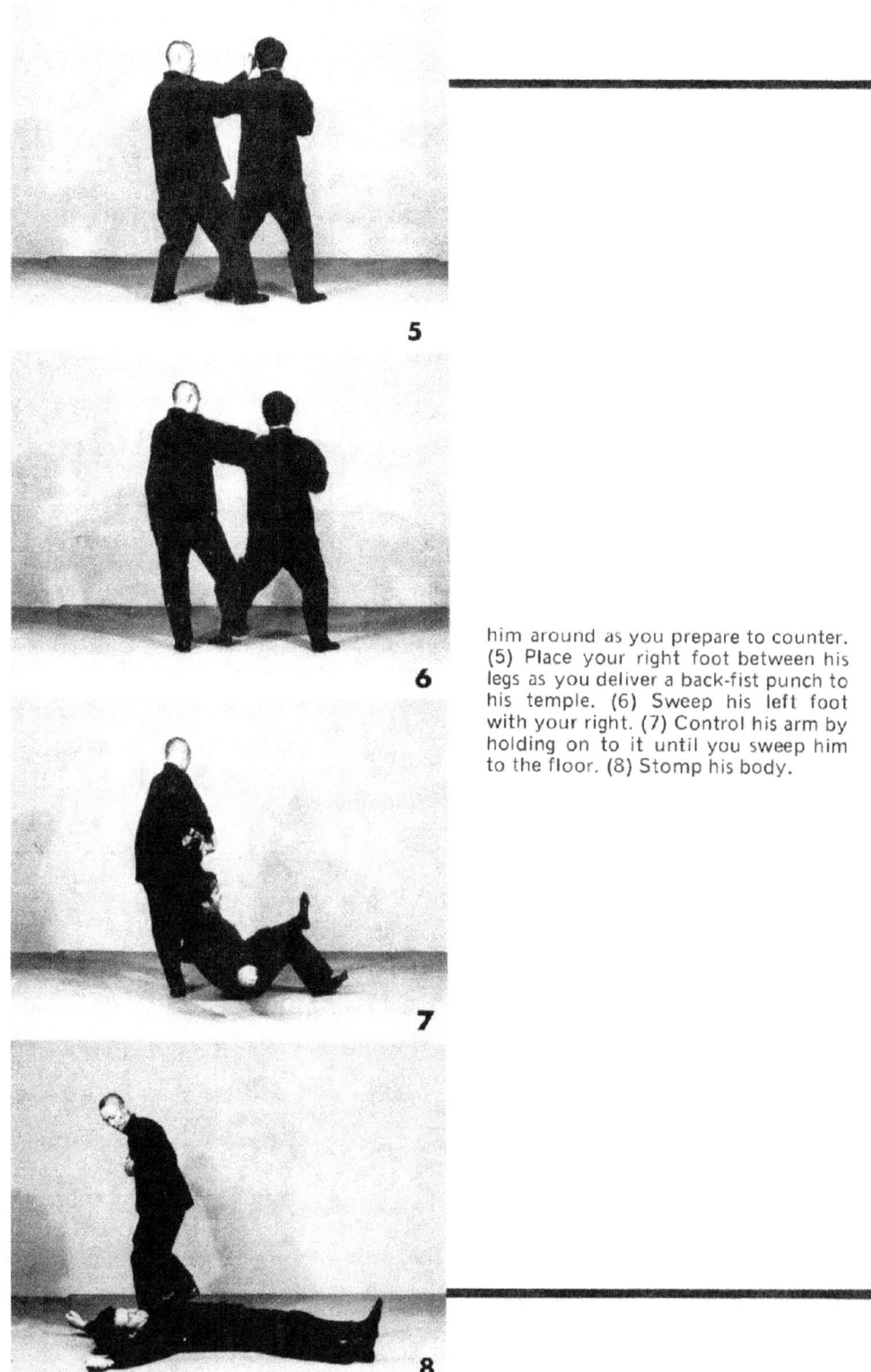

him around as you prepare to counter. (5) Place your right foot between his legs as you deliver a back-fist punch to his temple. (6) Sweep his left foot with your right. (7) Control his arm by holding on to it until you sweep him to the floor. (8) Stomp his body.

Left Jab Block and Counter

(1) Stand in a ready position with both hands up and your left foot forward. (2) If you attempt a left jab, and your opponent blocks it, (3) grab his wrist and step toward him. (4) Place your right foot next to his left

The Chinese Art of Self-Defense

foot to prevent him from kicking. (5) Before he has a chance to throw a cannon punch, raise your right hand to meet it. (6) Push his elbow into his face to throw him off balance. (7) Scoop his front leg with your foot, forcing him to the floor. (8) Kick to his body.

Left-Right Combination Defense

(1) Stand in a ready position with both hands up and your left foot forward. (2) As your opponent punches with his left, raise both your hands simultaneously, using your right hand to block his left hand and (3) your left hand to jab into his eyes. (4) Move closer in to block his right punch with your left hand, and execute a finger jab to his throat with your right hand.

Cross-Slap and Right Punch Defense

(1) Stand in a ready position with both hands up and your left foot forward. (2) As your opponent slaps your left hand to distract you and (3) throws a right punch to your face, releasing your left hand, block by raising your hand quickly. (4) Counter by moving toward him, and prepare to throw a vertical punch. (5) Direct your blow to his chin.

Right Lunge Punch Cross Block

(1) Stand in a ready position with both hands up and your left foot forward. (2) As opponent starts to throw a lunge punch, prepare to step in quickly with your right foot, raising your right arm to execute an inside block. (3)

The Chinese Art of Self-Defense

Step in and block. (4) Force his arm downward so he is open for a finger jab. (5) Execute the finger jab to his face with your left hand. (6) Return your right hand to the side. (7) Prepare for a cannon punch. (8) Apply the cannon punch to his solar plexus.

SIL LUM KUNG-FU

Back Fist Block and Counter

(1) Stand in a ready position with both hands up and your left foot forward. (2) Prepare to meet the opponent's back-fist attack by moving your right foot next to your left. (3) As he attempts to punch, take a short step forward with your right foot, simultaneously raising your right hand to

The Chinese Art of Self-Defense

block the blow before it reaches you. (4) Move closer to him and at the same time place your left hand under his elbow to immobilize him. (5) Draw your right hand back. (6) From a horse stance you can counter with a reverse punch to the kidney and then (7) draw your hand back again to (8) apply another punch to the head.

Left-Right Punch Defense

(1) Stand in a ready position with both hands up and your left foot forward. (2) As soon as your opponent throws a left punch, block it with your left wrist. (3) When he begins

The Chinese Art of Self-Defense

4

to counter with a right punch, (4) block him by twisting your palm toward him. (5) Grab his arm as you raise your right foot. (6) Apply a roundhouse kick to his temple.

5

6

Foot Sweep Defense and Counter

(1) Stand in a ready position with both hands up and your left foot forward. (2) Wait for your opponent to make the first move. (3) In this case he begins to apply a foot sweep. (4) Immediately lift your front foot high. (5) Counter with a cannon, or vertical, punch.

Slap and Right Punch Defense

(1) Stand in an opposite ready position with your right foot forward. (2) As your opponent slaps your right hand to immobilize it and (3) attempts to throw a straight, or right-hand, punch, move into him, simultaneously raising your left hand to block the blow and drawing your right hand to your hip. (4) Throw a reverse punch (5) to his solar plexus.

Front Kick Defense and Counter

(1) Stand in a ready position with both hands up and your left foot forward. (2) Wait for your opponent to make the first move. In this case he begins to apply a front kick. (3) Block his kick with the

The Chinese Art of Self-Defense

4

5

back of your left hand and prepare to grab his foot. Be sure that you just meet his blow and do not ward it off. (4) Grab his foot with both hands. (5) Twist it clockwise, forcing him over. (6) Apply a kick to the groin.

6

Left Jab Defense and Sweep

(1) Stand in a ready position with both hands up and your left foot forward. (2) As your opponent throws a left jab to your face, move your left hand to block it. (3) Grab his arm with your left hand. (4) Move closer to him,

1

2

3

4

placing your right foot behind his left. (5) Apply a finger jab with the right hand to his temple. (6) Immediately grab his left arm with your right and sweep his left leg. (7) Prepare for a spin kick. (8) Apply the spin kick to his chest area.

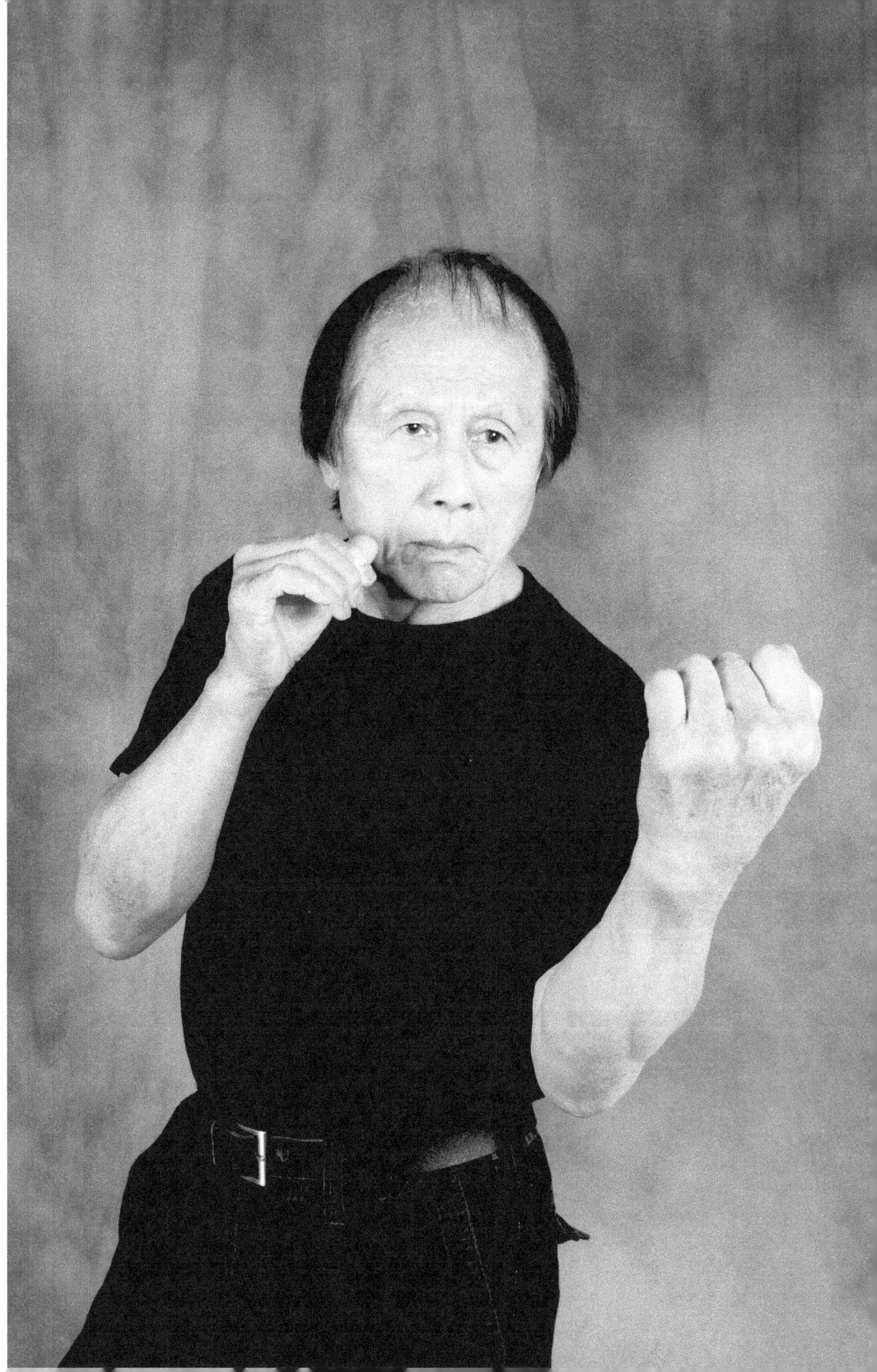

LEO T. FONG

The Evolution of the Integrated Fist
by Adam James

Long before people thought of the name Mixed Martial Arts, one man already was mastering the total approach to free fighting. There were others who combined techniques and created eclectic styles, but no one had integrated the basic fighting tools into one combat strategy that allows the fighter to move effortlessly and respond like a sound and an echo.

In the early 1970s, Leo Fong created Wei Kuen Do, which literally means the Way of the Integrated Fist. He was inspired by his friend and colleague Bruce Lee to create his own fighting system based on his unique knowledge and skills in the martial arts. Leo had been living in the Bay Area and training in a variety of Kung Fu systems and other Martial Arts but he always had been a boxer at heart. Whenever he was asked to spar, he would forget about whatever particular style he was supposed to be training in that day and instead would fight like a boxer, but with the additional skills of kicking and grappling.

An American martial arts pioneer, Leo has spent a lifetime pursuing excellence. Born in Canton, China, Leo moved to rural Arkansas at five years old and grew up during the Depression. Surrounded by strife, he fought back against the racism and challenges of life in a new country. While his father told him stories of the Kung Fu masters back in China, there were no Martial Arts schools anywhere nearby, so he turned to the American fighting systems. At this time in the United States, boxing was the number one sport and Arkansas was the home to many champions. He trained with several top teachers and became an AAU and Golden Gloves champion in Arkansas and Texas.

After receiving his Masters Degree in Theology from Southern Methodist University, Leo moved to Sacramento, California, to work as a minister. He began training in Jujitsu with Bill Luke, a top black belt under American Jujitsu pioneer Bruce Tegner, and in Judo under Bob Bendix. During this time, Leo worked hard to master the skills of grappling, choking, and joint breaking. He also studied the Korean martial art style Moo Duk Kwan-Tang Soo Do and developed dynamic kicks and striking techniques.

Next, Leo began to travel into San Francisco's Chinatown and sought out the best Kung Fu grandmasters. There he met T.Y. Wong, one of the city's premier teachers of Sil Lum Kung Fu and Lau Bun, the pioneer of Choy Lay Fut in America, and Leo trained with them extensively. Leo had a revelation one afternoon during a workout with one of the top students of Choy Lay Fut when they agreed to spar. The grandmaster forbade free fighting but the two decided to have a full contact fight before practice. During the session, the other man did his traditional Kung Fu techniques but Leo used boxing modified with the Martial Arts skills of kicking and grappling. It was no contest as Leo used the "stick and move" approach to circle around the man rooted in a horse stance with jabs, hooks, and occasional low kicks.

Leo used the principles of free fighting and blended the strikes of boxing, the kicks of Korean Martial Arts, the trapping of Wing Chun, the grappling of Judo/Jujitsu, the energetic training of Tai Chi/Chi Kung and, over time, the footwork and infighting of Filipino Martial Arts. He always adhered to the foundation of boxing and its emphasis on spontaneous action. Leo was deeply influenced by a number of brilliant masters and grandmasters of the Martial Arts, but deep inside he remained connected to the boxing experience of his youth.

Bruce Lee encouraged Leo to break away from traditional Martial Arts systems and to discover the outstanding martial artist that resided within him. Bruce espoused the virtues of being self-taught and relying on the basic skills of combat that Leo already possessed. Unfortunately, Bruce did not live long enough to define his philosophical approach to combat and create a curriculum that would allow the practitioner to develop these skills. However, Leo was given the key to liberate himself and developed a complete training approach for free fighting – moving beyond theory and discovering the path of excellence.

One evening, Bruce asked Leo a question that would change his life forever. Bruce was aware that Leo was training in a variety of martial arts. At the time, Leo was studying Tang Soo Do, Judo/Jujitsu, Sil Lum Kung Fu with TY Wong, Choy Lay Fut Kung Fu with Lao Bun, lifting weights with Bill Pearl, training with the Sacramento State boxing team, and working out with Bruce and Jimmy. So Bruce asked him bluntly, "Why are you running around town training with all of these guys?" Leo replied, "I'm looking for the ultimate." Bruce then said, "Man, there's no ultimate style … the ultimate is inside of you." and reached out and tapped Leo on the chest as he said this. It reminded Leo of the line in the Bible, "The Kingdom of God is within" (Luke 17:21).

Bruce told Leo that his boxing skills were "where it's at" and that he only needed to integrate the Wing Chun trapping, Judo/Jujitsu grappling, and the Tang Soo Do kicks to be the total package. He also said that he didn't believe that there was a secret technique in the traditional Martial Arts and that he was discovering the value of the aliveness in boxing and free fighting. Furthermore, Bruce expounded on the philosophy of self-realization – that a human being is more important than a Martial Arts style and that a person will know instinctively what is true and right.

During their time together, Leo also influenced Bruce, specifically in regard to boxing and a spontaneous approach to fighting. While living in Oakland, Bruce explored many other fighting methods, and he was particularly fascinated with boxing. He purchased 8mm films of the champion boxers of history and watched the films earnestly. At this time, Leo already was very experienced in boxing from the American amateur boxing program and whenever Leo was visiting, Bruce would pull out his boxing films and they would watch them for hours. Leo would tell Bruce all about the famous boxers and their styles, techniques, and training methods because he had grown up as a fan and student of the game.

Bruce, Leo, and Jimmy Lee frequently would have meetings to discuss and dissect the other Martial Arts styles and leading practitioners. The three of them always found flaws in the styles that lacked the aliveness and spontaneity of free fighting systems like boxing, wrestling, and Judo. They also disliked those who practiced a variety of styles and attempted to do all of the techniques possible, instead of perfecting the basic tools of combat and the subtleties of a single technique. Another turning point in Bruce's appreciation for the boxing approach to Martial Arts occurred during his famous fight with Wong Jack Man. Even though he had won the fight, Bruce was very disappointed with his performance. He was frustrated that he couldn't hit Wong cleanly and that his straight blast was ineffective.

Immediately after the fight, Jimmy called Leo on the phone and told him about the outcome. Then, Jimmy handed the phone to Bruce and he told Leo that he was very upset that he couldn't hit Wong cleanly. Leo said, "You need to throw hooks and uppercuts - use more angles." The next time Leo visited Bruce, he was hitting a heavy bag and using boxing techniques - a jab, hook, cross, and uppercut. Bruce was moving around on the balls of his feet and using the "stick and move" tactic. Leo could see that Bruce had begun a transformation and was starting to tap into the freedom and spontaneity of boxing punches.

Over time, Leo began to perfect his personal approach to fighting and developed his own expression of Martial Arts. However, he never thought to put a label to his new style and didn't give it a name. Then, while on a business trip to Hong Kong, Leo got together with Bruce's childhood friend Unicorn Chan, and also Chaplin Chang, the assistant director of the film Enter the Dragon. One afternoon, Leo and Chaplin were riding in a cab as they were going to a meeting with the editor of Hong Kong's number one Martial Arts magazine for an interview. While driving there, Chaplin was asking Leo about his experiences with Bruce and his own personal Martial Arts style. Leo told Chaplin that out of respect to Bruce he did not call what he did Jeet Kune Do and that he really didn't have a name for it. He explained to Chaplin that he combined boxing with several styles of Kung Fu, including Wing Chun, Choy Lay Fut, and Sil Lum and that he also integrated the kicking of Tang Soo Do and the grappling of Judo/Jujitsu.

Chaplin thought for a moment and said, "You should call your style Wei Kuen Do." Leo said "What does that mean?" and Chaplin explained that it means "The way of the integrated fist." Leo told Chaplin that he really liked the name because it reflected his connection to Bruce but it also was his own truth. He went on to tell Chaplin that he also liked the name because he had grown up in the Southeastern United States during segregation and believes in the concept of integration. Leo appreciated how the name emphasized a process of assimilating various forces and then blending them into one complete force, and he could see how this name reflected the process that he and Bruce had been pursuing. Bruce often had talked about how styles caused separation and limitation and that the "ultimate style" was a personal expression of the totality of free fighting.

In 1976, Leo Fong wrote the book "Wei Kuen Do: the Psychodynamic Art of Free Fighting" and he documented the basics of his new approach to fighting. He stated in the preface that his book was not meant to be a technical manual but rather a text on the art of expressing oneself spontaneously in a combat situation. Furthermore, he explained that free fighting requires more than technical skills and brings into play the mind, emotions, and spirit. The dynamics of free fighting is a process – a personal journey – and the practitioner must consider the psychic aspect of fighting. He noted that the important ingredients that make a winner – such as timing, distance, body rhythm, mental awareness, concentration, and relaxed focus – are mental attributes that make the techniques work, and that without them, technical skills are just empty movements. Leo emphasized that it doesn't matter if the palm is down when you punch or to the side, but only that it is executed at the right time and that it lands on the target.

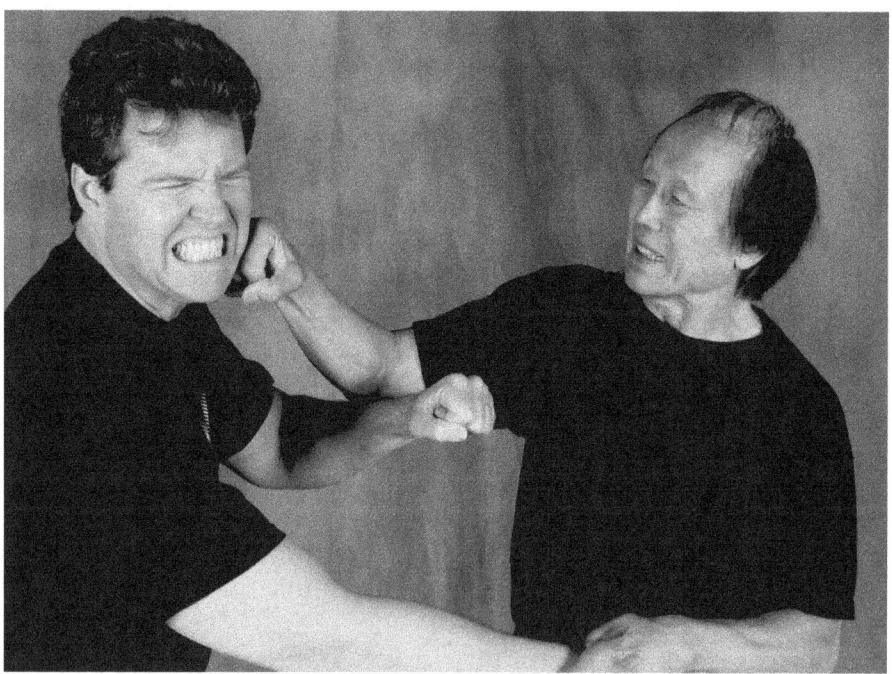

The Chinese Art of Self-Defense

Wei Kuen Do therefore is a term describing a process, and Leo wrote that the skills of free fighting couldn't be handed on a platter. The instructor only can show the direction one must travel but the dedicated practitioner must develop the mental, emotional, and spiritual skills. Leo dedicated the book to those who are searching for the upper levels of training and the self--truth in relation to combat.

To this end, Leo included in the book a quote from the philosopher Kahlil Gibran – "No man can reveal to you aught but that which already lies asleep in the dawning of your knowledge. The teacher who walks in the shadow of the temple, among his followers, gives not of his wisdom but rather of his faith and his lovingness. If he is indeed wise he does not bid you enter the house of his wisdom, but rather leads you to the threshold of your own mind."

Leo refined the skills of Wei Kuen Do to an even higher level and composed a series of combinations that reveal the essence of excellence to the practitioner. Through training in these techniques and drills, the practitioner will discover the four stages of development for free fighting – 1) Developing the tools; 2) Refining the tools; 3) Dissolving the tools; and 4) Expressing the tools. The final level is complete freedom in combat and spontaneous right action.

The physical structure of Wei Kuen Do is similar to a boxing stance with the emphasis on light, quick tactical footwork. The techniques are the basic strikes of boxing such as the jab, hook, cross, and uppercut. However, Leo also incorporated the energetic "feel" of Kung Fu with trapping gleamed from Wing Chun and leg attacks from kickboxing. While grappling is included, the strategy of Wei Kuen Do is to avoid takedowns and maintain distance – so that the fighter can use the footwork to move and position himself to "hit without getting hit."

One of the unique aspects of Wei Kuen Do is the footwork, which includes the "V-step" or triangle step integrated from Filipino knife fighting. After several decades of training in Modern Arnis with Remy Presas and Serrada Escrima with Angel Cabales, Leo created his own approach to knife and stick fighting called Modern Escrima. However, he also integrated the V-step into his open hand fighting techniques and developed special punching combinations that make use of this dynamic footwork. The punches are synchronized with the footwork and the fighter will step and hit at the same time. Old-time boxers like Sam Langford and Benny Leonard often used this technique, which is commonly called "switch hitting" in boxing circles. Many boxing trainers don't like this type of hitting, but some of the best modern boxers – such as Manny Pacquiao and Floyd Mayweather, Jr. – use it to baffle their opponents. Leo didn't stop there and also gleaned footwork from basketball to enhance fighting positioning. In particular, Leo studied Kobe Bryant and the crossover dribble step to evolve faking techniques and take them to a new level.

Leo also developed a new training program based on energy exercises, Martial Arts techniques, and weight training. As he began to integrate Chi Kung and Tai Chi training with modern weight training techniques, he created a revolutionary system of exercise that develops functional strength, stamina, and natural self-defense movement patterns. The system uses lightweight dumbbells, the energy training of Martial Arts, and deep breathing, and it leads to an incredible increase in strength, endurance, and internal energy. At first, Leo called the new system "Chi Kuen Do" (the way of the energy fist), but he renamed it "Chi Fung," which means "energy breath/wind," which reflects both his emphasis on deep breathing and also his original family name of Fung.

However, what makes Wei Kuen Do unique is the emphasis on the process of character development and the ultimate focus is on building the champion within. Cus D'Amato, the great boxing trainer, often talked about the importance of character to make a great champion and that the "will to win" is greater than the "skill to win." Leo was asked to give a seminar to the Machado Brothers' students and he taught the life skills of Martial Arts training. He told them that you can't choke out depression and you can't submit death, and that the true mark of a winner is overcoming the three D's – disease, divorce, and death. Through the training of the mind, spirit, and emotions, Leo created the Wei Kuen Do curriculum of the Life Warrior program.

In 2006, Leo Fong was recognized as the founder of three

The Chinese Art of Self-Defense

unique martial arts styles – Wei Kuen Do, Modern Escrima and Chi Fung. However, Leo prefers to look at these three systems as part of the whole, and they are, in fact, integrated together. Wei Kuen Do is free fighting; Modern Escrima simply extends the hand with a weapon; and Chi Fung is the strength training system that complements the totality. As a result, the training of all three will repeat specific movement patterns that in turn develop muscle memory and therefore spontaneous action in combat. Instead of segregating multiple Martial Arts styles and strength training systems, which will lead to confusion and hesitation, Leo integrated the basic tools into one complete approach that will engender excellence.

The end result is complete and whole, and it comes from the result of internal integration and then spontaneous, natural action. This is the ultimate result of mixing martial arts – the integrated fist.

www.ingramcontent.com/pod-product-compliance
Lightning Source LLC
Chambersburg PA
CBHW080443090526
44586CB00047B/2268